Prophetic
Evangelism

*kingdom exploits
in the risk zone*

First published in Great Britain by
Christian Publications International ("CPI")
an imprint of Inspiration – Assurance Publications
PO Box 212 Saffron Walden CB10 2UU UK

ISBN 978-1-913741-06-8
Prophetic Evangelism – Kingdom Exploits Risk Zone
Edn 2 (Dan Holland)

Printed in Great Britain by Imprint Digital, Exeter
and worldwide by Ingram-Spark

DEDICATION

'Whom have I in heaven but you?
And earth has nothing I desire besides you.'
Psalm 73v 25

With a heart brimming over with gratitude
I dedicate this book to my Lord, Saviour, friend,
elder brother and captain, Jesus Christ.
I love You with all of my heart,
You are my everything.
Thank You for the mysterious adventure
of discipleship, and the incredible saints
You have introduced me to.
Thank You for trusting me with Your gospel
and allowing me to live for Your glory.
Be lifted up in this book; it's all Your work.
Please breathe through it to inspire,
provoke, encourage and to teach.

WITH THANKS

Grateful thanks to my wonderful wife, Bec, and amazing daughter, Anna, for all the sacrifices you have made.

Thank you to the TFM family; Tim and Georgina, Paul and Paula, David B, David C, Denise, Tao and many others. Bless you for your passion for souls and humility of heart.

Thank you Gordon and Gill for your example in local church evangelism. You introduced me to, and encourage me to live, life in the Spirit.

Thank you Peter for your generous belief in, and steady hand over, this project. Thanks Chris for your invaluable attention to detail, and your prayers.

Michael, bless you for the lovely layout.

IN MEMORY OF

David Henfrey, Dec 1955 to Aug 2017.
A lovely Christian brother,
whose gracious legacy funded this
and other Christian books.

To God be the glory ...

Foreword

As I write this Foreword the church is living through the strangest days – the period after the lockdown caused by the Coronavirus. Every church is deciding whether to re-open for worship, and, if so, what restrictions, rules and regulations must be followed.

Against this background, the question of what the church is for becomes paramount – and within that, the place of evangelism.

For decades much 'ink has been spilt' trying to persuade Christians to evangelise... to tell their friends, neighbours and strangers they encounter about their faith. And generally speaking, books, courses and leaflets set out to make evangelism easy, to make it simple, so people may be encouraged and get involved. A laudable aim, however it risks reducing evangelism to a formula. It can all too easily become human centred rather than God centred.

This book offers something different. It begins with the idea that God Himself has something He wants to say – and that He wishes to use us to be His 'mouthpiece'.

And this changes everything – for it relieves the pressure people sometimes feel that they have to say something about their faith – which so often results in the embarrassment of an unnatural or forced encounter. Instead it asks us to spend time on our relationship with our Father God, that we may hear more clearly from Him. Then we shall be able to speak or act His word in a way that transforms situations and brings the opportunity of a real conversation about faith.

I've been involved with Through Faith Missions in one way or another for over 25 years. Now, as in years past, God works as much in our team members as in the places where we are working – and its been a privilege to work alongside Dan over this last year or two. This book, and Dan's knowledge and gifting, are extremely valuable in reminding us of, and drawing us back into, the prophetic; to that moment when God Himself breaks into a human life, or into a situation.

I commend it to you. And may God bless you as you read.

Rev Tim Hall
CEO Through Faith Missions

Contents

Introduction

'Don't you have a saying, 'It's still four months until harvest'? I tell you, open your eyes and look at the fields! They are ripe for harvest'. (John 4v 35)

She was hunched, red eyed and distracted, a woman in her thirties. I fought my way across the manic rush hour in King's Cross station. I was weary, glad to be on my way home and looking forward to sitting down on the train with my newspaper. London has a way of tiring me out. In amongst all the hustle and bustle, I went past a seating area where my attention was drawn to this particular lady.

She was highlighted to me somehow, sitting down on a bench. It felt like I was walking through quicksand as I approached her, my pulse rapid and my mind rebelling against what I was about to do. I knew I had to say something to her. How I knew, I don't know? I was absolutely sure. What should I say? As I slowed down my mind worked on this, it would be a 'drive-by' word. I leant over to make it clear I wanted to talk to her and the words that tumbled out were *'God has not forgotten you!'* I gulped, it came out with confidence. I now stood a realistic chance of being told to f-off in front of lots of commuters.

Who knows what she was going through to be crying so publicly at the station? This was not one tear rolling down her cheek as she sat staring "out of a train window", but rather she was abandoned to her pain. It was something that over-rode the customary English reserve. Was she leaving her husband or vice versa? Running away from something, maybe even God and feeling lost and bereft? Full of remorse at something she had done? I could speculate, but only God knew. It was an encounter of mere seconds.

Through the haze of her tears she mouthed *'thank-you'* and weakly once again *'thank-you'*, looking me in the eyes. I smiled in genuine relief, said God bless you, and was on my way. Those few words clearly did mean something to her. Were they simply an expression of Christian compassion as I could see her raw grief? No there was something more, a flicker of understanding in her eyes; a prophetic edge to it.

Why would I say to someone that 'God's not forgotten you'? It's only significant if that person has some understanding of, or relationship with,

God. I had no way of knowing that naturally. Maybe she was a 'prodigal' daughter expecting the hammer blow of God's judgement. Through me she received a kindly reminder that her heavenly father looks for her return every day from his balcony. Or maybe those words were the equivalent of 'does no-body condemn you? Then neither do I, go and sin no more.' (John 8 v10-11) We do our small part and trust God to do His large and often unseen part. I did pray as I sat on my train but that was the last time I remembered her until years later.

As I travel around churches in my work as evangelist, I see the struggle to make disciples and the frustration at how few conversions are happening. Often it seems a massive challenge to get people talking about Jesus, let alone making commitments to Him. Some churches are shrinking as people die or leave.

Our postmodern culture is less interested in our doctrine and more concerned about spirituality and acceptance. Absolutes, especially moral absolutes, are viewed with hostility and resentment. Extremely high value is placed on personal 'freedom' and 'truth'. Methods of evangelism that worked well in decades past don't seem to be having the same impact now, and at worst can be counterproductive.

Prophetic evangelism flows from living in vital connection with God. We hear and see what God is doing, with a heart to join in. It involves being available to God at any moment to speak, move, lay hands on, pray and witness to whomever we are guided. This means being vulnerable to God and to other people in ways that are exciting and terrifying. It necessitates our relationship with God deepening and widening in intimacy and trust.

As God's children we want to be equipped and we aim to be ready. We long to see the lost saved. For this we need as many tools in our evangelistic toolbox as possible. Prophetic evangelism is just one more tool in that toolbox. I make no claims that it is 'the' answer to all evangelistic frustrations, or the woes of our society, but it will reward us to investigate it. Maybe it is at least part of the answer?

I do believe there is a 'nowness' about prophetic evangelism. This is a powerful tool Jesus has sovereignly gifted to His Church in this hour and the time is ripe to bring in the harvest. It's time to pioneer again. Our glorious gospel is not chained, and we don't apologise for it; but we do need new ways to unleash it into hearts, minds, communities, and cultures. If we have a will to share our beautiful Jesus with our friends, families and communities we can rest assured God will give us a way.

Prophetic evangelism is an approach to sharing the good news of Jesus (evangelism) using specifically those prophetic tools and gifting provided by the Holy Spirit to those evangelising. The message delivered by prophetic evangelism is (almost always) God's way of directly challenging an individual causing them to recognize a definitive decision point in their life.

The message never changes, but the methods need to. We are filled with the Holy Spirit, the creative power and wisdom of God. Maybe we need to come to Him with a blank canvas to dream again! We evangelise – or we fossilize. Revival is always preceded by repentance in God's people who humble themselves and cry out to hear His voice again at any cost.

Maybe the forms of evangelism you've witnessed before terrify you; this method might just liberate your inner evangelist who's never emerged before! This might be the mantle that is made to measure for you. At the very least it will give you understanding for those who operate in this way. Do you have reservations about prophecy? Please prayerfully reserve judgement until you've shared some of my journey and discoveries. You may identify with my ups and downs. I've experienced the good, the bad and the ugly of charismatic Christianity and prophecy.

Whether or not you are an evangelist and/or prophetically gifted, prophetic evangelism is a tool that we may all use on occasion to a greater or lesser extent, consciously – and perhaps even unconsciously. My prayer is that this book might inspire, stir, challenge, equip and excite you with the possibilities of outreach.

'The harvest is plentiful but the workers are few. Ask the Lord of the harvest, therefore, to send out workers into his harvest field.' (Matt 9v 37a–38)

Prophetic Evangelism

kingdom exploits in the risk zone

Part 1

The Evangelism Imperative

1 The Great Commission

This magnificent com-mission belongs to us, the weighty last command and heartcry of Jesus, our Saviour, captain and chief apostle. We were chosen for this day, *'And who knows but that you have come to your royal position for such a time as this?"* (Est 4v 14). This is our appointed moment to shine, what we do now will resound into eternity. Jesus invites us (actually it's a command) to pick up the 'mission' baton with which His disciples have run for 2000 years. It's our time and it's our turn. Shall we be the generation that completes the great commission? This noble gauntlet lies at our feet, thrown there by previous generations. Will we pick it up and run with the mission and message of Christ? All of heaven awaits our decision. If we don't aim for something, we'll achieve nothing. Much hangs on our decision.

'Then Jesus came to them and said, "All authority in heaven and on earth has been given to me. Therefore go and make disciples of all nations, baptizing them in the name of the Father and of the Son and of the Holy Spirit, and teaching them to obey everything I have commanded you. And surely I am with you always, to the very end of the age."
(Matt 28v 18- 20)

We are messengers bearing the victorious news of that stone rolled away, of our risen Lord. We pound the streets, traversing the earth, telling every tribe and tongue, people and nation that Jesus has triumphed. He has conquered our ancient foe, the accuser of the brethren. He has defeated death, swallowed up the grave and paid in His blood for our forgiveness so that we can know God as Father. Every street, hamlet, village, town, city and nation must be told, and then the end will surely come (Matt 24v 14). We are closer than we have ever been, what exciting times we live in. How glorious is our call to proclaim the return of the victorious king. Let's return to the joy of our gospel (Psalm 51v 12), become highly conversant in it and skilful when sharing it.

Have you ever wondered why we aren't taken up to heaven when we give our lives to Jesus? Why not depart this world with all its woes and worship Him forever? We remain here to proclaim His glory. We have the privilege of telling people, He did this for me, He can do the same for you. It's a simple, beautiful, and profound testimony backed up by the transformation people observe in our lives. Why would we keep such superb news to ourselves, it'd be wrong, wouldn't it? We've found the water of life in a desert where we're surrounded by people dying of thirst. We've found beautiful food in a famine when people are starving to death. We have the antivenom to a deadly snake bite that everyone is dying of.

The gospel is good news for all of humanity; rich and poor, sick and healthy, sinner and saint, black and white, young and old (Gal 3v 28). God wants His message to reach into the furthest corners of the world with its cleansing, healing, and redemptive power. It's extraordinary that with all our technology and the ease of travel that we, the church, still haven't fulfilled the great commission after 2000 years. This can change if we take ourselves and God seriously.

So far we can all agree, but at this point many of us waver and disqualify ourselves. Our concept of evangelism is narrow and frightening. We can think that if we're not Billy Graham, Reinhard Bonnke or J.John then we are not to do evangelism. We wrestle with this for a while and then we give up. We accept that dull ache of guilt somewhere in the background because we know we should be doing something. Or we screw ourselves up for excruciating ministry that in reality we aren't called to.

'How, then, can they call on the one they have not believed in? And how can they believe in the one of whom they have not heard? And how can they hear without someone preaching to them?'
(Romans 10v 14)

Think of the people you've seen on the High Street with a PA and sandwich board, red faced, both terrified and terrifying. They don't have a preaching gift or communication skills but they more than compensate with guts. The problem is some of us think that this caricature is our only option if we're going to 'do' evangelism.

The enemy has been so successful at reducing 'evangelism' to the activity of a few 'experts'. They are run ragged, criss-crossing the globe while the rest of the church sits safely inside the church building. We must break out of this perverse model of evangelism. It's the church in entirety that can fulfil the Great Commission. Because you're not an out and out (Ephesians 4) evangelist, and few are, it doesn't mean you can't do any evangelism.

"It is the whole job of the whole church to preach the whole gospel to the whole world'
(C.H.Spurgeon)

We mustn't allow ourselves to be sidelined. If we have a will there's a way for us, we can find our niche and start to flourish. There's a huge spectrum where we can participate, thrive, and get an appetite for evangelism. There's nothing healthier and more life affirming for us than sharing Jesus. It's addictive in a good way. Let's rediscover the 'GO' of the gospel.

'He said to them, "Go into all the world and preach the gospel to all

creation. Whoever believes and is baptized will be saved, but whoever does not believe will be condemned. And these signs will accompany those who believe: In my name they will drive out demons; they will speak in new tongues; they will pick up snakes with their hands; and when they drink deadly poison, it will not hurt them at all; they will place their hands on sick people, and they will get well." (Mark 16v 15-18)

Every Christian is bound to be a missionary, even though he be not ordained as a preacher. The spirit of missions is the spirit of Christ, and when the whole Church is imbued with that the Lord's prayer will be answered, "Thy kingdom come."
(E.P. Rogers, D.D.)

2 *Methods of evangelism*

As we celebrate some different types of evangelism you'll realise you've been doing far more than you thought. There are so many brilliant ways we can share our Saviour Jesus, high and low intensity, direct and oblique. There's always a way. There isn't a hierarchy of methods, one is not inherently better than others; it's a case of horses for courses. God will lead us to the one which is best for our circumstance.

Friendship Evangelism

This method has been extremely popular in recent times and there is a plethora of books and training resources. Its simple beauty involves intentionally investing in existing and new *‘Come and see a man who told me everything I ever did’* (John 4v 29) friendships. These are watered with prayer over time with the aim of bringing that person to Christ. It's *‘come and see’* as Philip said to Nathaniel; we might invite our friends to come with us to an event or service.

The tension in this approach is that the 'friendship' can supersede the intended evangelism and after years of lovely conversations there's still no confrontation about the cross, and no salvation. The friendship can be so nourishing that we don't want to rock the boat with the offence of the gospel.

On the other hand, Christian 'friendship' is hypocritical when we ditch someone because they have had long enough to decide and 'won't become a Christian anyway'. If you think this is far-fetched, I've met people on the other side of this scenario. They were befriended and finally decided to 'come' to church; at which point they were 'dropped'. They concluded bitterly that they weren't interesting anymore because they'd joined the club. The evangelist had moved on to the next project. We must avoid at all costs this agenda driven style of 'friendship,' without sacrificing the gospel. If our friends never come to Christ, they need to know we'll still be there for them.

When I was away from church, I had friends who always opened their home to me; they fed me beautiful food and listened to some of my struggles. I'm sure they never stopped praying, and although they occasionally mentioned church there was no pressure to come back. Their unspoken 'gospel' of friendship was a hundred times more powerful.

Media Evangelism

'Sow your seed in the morning, and at evening let your hands not be idle, for you do not know which will succeed, whether this or that, or whether both will do equally well'.
(Eccles 11v 6)

Think of the unprecedented time of lockdown Britain faced with the Coronavirus in 2020. Many people who had never been on Facebook, including myself, took the plunge. I'm already hooked on engagements, shares and tags. I need my dopamine fix! Services are happening all over the world on Zoom and all sorts of new evangelistic approaches are emerging. Truly 'necessity is the mother of invention'. Short videos, tweets, vlogs, blogs and webinars. The technology is neutral, it's what we do with it that counts and whether it controls us, or vice versa.

Media offers the opportunity to 'broadcast' the seed of the gospel, to cast it far and wide, we just don't know who it reaches. It's a forum where people who want to investigate Christianity from a safe distance can do so. However, there might be flaky stuff online that isn't helpful. We must pray that people make it past 'virtual' Christianity and on-line church to meeting real, live, imperfect Christians who aren't airbrushed on Instagram. Media can grab the short attention span of the average person in the hopes of focusing it on Jesus and His teaching. Let's hope people find their way into church and the reality isn't too much of a shock for them after the gloss of media blogs and video.

Power (presence) Evangelism

'They had come from every village of Galilee and from Judea and Jerusalem. And the power of the Lord was with Jesus to heal the sick'.
(Luke 5v 17b)

This method offers people an opportunity to experience the power of the living God. You may have heard of or participated in 'healing on the streets' and 'healing rooms'. We lean into God's love for the lost and desire to reach them. Someone who receives a powerful healing, and friends and family who witness this, might then pay attention to the message which otherwise they'd have ignored.

Having been involved in this style of evangelism myself, it's disconcerting if God doesn't obviously 'show up'. Faith is spelt R.I.S.K., God keeps us on our toes. We can assume that if we had more healings, we'd get more salvations. I've witnessed a healing miracle happening to a person at an open air service, who afterwards never came to church once, and carried on with their own life. It's disappointing because we assume they'll be a Christian once they've experienced God. After all, many turned away from Jesus when the miracles and food were followed up with teaching (John 6v 67). Nevertheless, I always want to see more healings, and rejoice when I do.

Incidentally, we only found out about the healing (mentioned above) by a 'chance' meeting months later in the street. Only one cleansed leper returned to thank Jesus, and he wasn't an Israelite (Luke 17v 11-19). Of course, we can be assured God continues working on a long term basis with these people.

Anecdotally, the Lost often get healed easier than believers, and our step of faith, praying expectantly, honours God. In power evangelism we're offering real solutions to real problems, which can be followed up by a Salvation opportunity. The message is, almost subliminally, 'that was Jesus on the outside; would you like to experience Jesus on the inside?' Today is the day of Salvation!

Invitational/Event Evangelism

Matthew the tax collector, newly a follower of Jesus, hosted a pot roast dinner for his friends to come and hear Jesus. We could host men's or women's breakfasts with a guest speaker or film nights with a short talk, themed evening etc. All ways to invite someone into a relaxed context to hear the gospel. It could be a guest speaker so those invited wouldn't think that anything is aimed directly at them. Also, they might be able to speak with the guest speaker more freely.

'While Jesus was having dinner at Matthew's house, many tax collectors and sinners came and ate with him and his disciples'. (Matt 9v 10)

We want to avoid people becoming 'special event addicts', going to one every three months but avoiding regular church life. Some people think they can survive on these events but they can't grow strong and won't become disciples.

I have preached a message in India to people who are sitting on the edge of their seats and lining up for prayer afterwards (and they mean serious prayer). I've spoken to an English congregation with folded arms, playing with phones and wandering in and out. It's generally true that an invited guest speaker can break down barriers of apathy that can defeat a local person. It's that classic but very true idea that 'familiarity breeds contempt'! A new voice reinforcing old truths can be helpful. Jesus Himself said,

"A prophet is not without honour except in his own town, among his relatives and in his own home." (Mark 6v 4)

Doorstep Evangelism

I've heard people say that door-knocking doesn't work anymore; I always want to ask them to tell me, then what is working? Obviously, sensitivity is required but at Through Faith Missions we see that door knocking, done well, really does work. Most Christians don't like doing it and therefore don't try it, so it's a self-fulfilling prophecy. They'll talk negatively about Jehovah's Witnesses and Mormons but the fact is that there are some people we'll reach like this that otherwise would be untouched. Through Faith Missions has thirty five years of testimonies to back this up.

We've had incredible conversations, many times culminating in the person receiving prayer. Occasionally things do go 'pear shaped', but if we can navigate the situation with grace, it's still a witness. Over a week's mission, the person who sent us away with a flea in our ear on day one will often bump into the team later in the week. A gracious response earlier makes it possible to have a fresh start later. They will remember we didn't lash back at them.

'If it is possible, as far as it depends on you, live at peace with everyone'. (Romans 12v 18)

One woman in Ireland was fit to spit at me, and it wasn't because I was impolite. As she slammed the door I managed to get a 'God bless you' through the crack, and I really felt in that moment that God was going to use it in her life. A strong reaction can be evidence of conviction.

'Here I am! I stand at the door and knock. If anyone hears my voice and opens the door, I will come in and eat with that person, and he with me'. (Rev 3v 20)

Academic Evangelism (Apologetics)

Paul then stood up in the meeting of the Areopagus and said: "People of Athens! I see that in every way you are very religious. (Acts 17v 22)

This demonstrates an understanding and implicit awareness of other religions and world-views. It's particularly helpful with students, academics and philosophers. It sharpens us to grapple with differences and contradictions. I knew of a Christian brought up in Pakistan who knew the Koran almost as well as the Bible. He was very effective in public debate with Muslims who were ill-prepared for his razor sharp apologetics.. It turns out many of them didn't know the Koran. I wonder how often that could be said about Christians and the Bible.

Apologetics can be an intellectual exercise and set up a winning/losing dynamic which we need to be mindful of when our message is love. We could 'win' a debate but 'lose' our audience. So we pray that the heart is also touched. Generally the head follows the heart, not the other way around. Many people have hearts that genuinely want their heads to be convinced!

The beauty of apologetics is that the Bible stands up to the most rigorous scrutiny. We have nothing to hide, and we can hold our ground in any debate. An accomplished Christian apologist can dismantle every argument against the gospel, at least for those with genuine desire for logic and truth.

"Every word of God is flawless" (Prov 30v 5)

Mass Evangelism

How many times have you heard it said that Billy Graham style mass evangelism doesn't work now? I'm not sure that's true, the jury's still out for me. People are more likely to turn out en mass to listen to someone with a national reputation than pastor Bobby in the local community centre.

We have 'home cinemas', Netflix, Xbox and Facebook; non-stop entertainment from morning to evening. The lure of a Christian 'crusade' may not be what it once was in the West but in Africa and Asia they're still going strong and will continue to do so.

This style of evangelism does make it easier to go forward for a 'commitment', with thousands at the same time, than at a Sunday morning service with fifteen people watching intently. Also, the volume of prayer back-up that is possible in a stadium event is hard to replicate in smaller settings. Mass evangelism offers the chance to preach to 'church goers' who are not 'Christians,' even if they think they are.

Follow-up is a challenge. Billy Graham had a very good organisation which always prepared local ministries, but through no fault of his, many converts slipped back into the world. With tens of thousands of decisions it would take brilliant administration to follow-up with each individual, even if they make themselves available. I had the privilege of leading someone to Christ at an Easter bandstand service; I knew where he lived and had his mobile number but despite extensive efforts I concluded sadly that he didn't want to be found, until years later when he surfaced again. This is just one person. Imagine chasing up thousands!

Short-Term Evangelism (Mission)

Luke 9 v 1-6 is arguably the first New Testament short term mission. After quite a short time observing Him, Jesus commissioned and sent out the twelve and then later the seventy two. I work for a missions agency (Through Faith Missions) and am honoured to do so, but if local churches

When Jesus had called the Twelve together, he gave them power and authority to drive out all demons and to cure diseases, and he sent them out to proclaim the kingdom of God and to heal the sick. He told them: "Take nothing for the journey—no staff, no bag, no bread, no money, no extra shirt. Whatever house you enter, stay there until you leave that town. If people do not welcome you, leave their town and shake the dust off your feet as a testimony against them."So they set out and went from village to village, proclaiming the good news and healing people everywhere'.
(Luke 9v 1–6)

were permanently missional, then over time para-church organisations might become obsolete. We are needed because mission is often "the sacrificial lamb" in churches, the first thing to be sacrificed. We live in the real world where a missional 'shot in the arm' is often required to kick-start churches into action. Sometimes a group from outside can say and do things that the vicar or pastor couldn't. It's also true that a focussed time of mission, where the tyranny of the urgent is suspended, is often when God births longer term evangelistic projects.

A good friend of mine in South London, Steve, was involved in stewarding at a mission on Streatham Common some six years ago. During the mission he met a homeless Russian man, sleeping in the bushes there. He suffered from PTSD and alcoholism and didn't have much English; Steve prayed for him before he disappeared forever. God moved on Steve's heart as he wondered how he would cope if he were in a similar position in Russia and the vision for a 'Community Table' was born.

Over time, and with prayer, this vision materialised as a homeless outreach based in his home church (Ichthus Southcroft). Community Table is open for four hours every Thursday, providing a delicious home cooked meal to some forty to fifty homeless and needy people with a volunteer staff of six to ten. Those attending are offered a shower, new clothes and as much prayer as they want. All sorts of outside agencies (drug and alcohol counselling, TB unit, housing support) visit because they know it is a reliable and safe place to meet. Most importantly the gospel is faithfully preached, every Thursday lunchtime for six years, even on Christmas day.

I had the privilege to work at the community table for a year and preached six or seven times. It was the highlight of my week. I have absolutely no doubt it was a God inspired idea with His blessing all over it. All of this sparked off from God speaking to Steve at a mission in Streatham in 2014. Could God have spoken to Steve anyway? Yes, probably, but it just so happened the idea came at a time of focussed mission. I have observed this providential pattern many times! We give Jesus our undivided attention, we actively care about what He cares about, and He will feed our imaginations.

It's a shame the energy and drive of short-term mission can't be replicated longer term. Some churches are exhausted just after hosting a team for a week. If the local church members don't engage then lasting fruit (ie. making disciples) may sadly be rare; it's unrealistic for the pastor to do all the follow up work. We must also avoid the attitude that 'we've done our evangelism for the year (or decade) now', after completing a mission.

'Your people will volunteer freely in the day of Your power'
(Psalm 110v 3b)

Finally, short term mission can be a great way to launch a church-plant. Rather like the construction teams that throw up a new supermarket in a matter of weeks; there's another team that carry on the day to day running of it, but they couldn't do that if the 'building' hadn't been prepared. Short term mission is the cavalry that breaks through the enemy ranks so that the whole army can march through and make camp in enemy territory.

Church-Planting Evangelism

Church planting is generally agreed to be the best and most sustainable method for local evangelism. It's dispiriting to have new converts disappear back into the woodwork without a trace. A church plant ready to disciple new believers can integrate people naturally into church life. If a new contact isn't fed into a local church how can s/he prosper? A church plant might be on the doorstep rather than six miles across town. Statistics show that a new convert is most effective in bringing other people into the Kingdom of God, with his or her existing friends and social networks. A church plant gives people the opportunity to contribute straight away.

"Planting new churches is the most effective evangelistic methodology known under heaven."
(C P Wagner)

A church plant has the 'seed' potential to befriend, evangelise, disciple, teach, pastor and train. It does not have all the maintenance issues, build-up of politics and inertia that older churches often struggle with. It's all hands-on deck. I've seen people grow extremely fast in this way; learning and doing, there's no need for it to take years and years. In the current church scene in the UK the church planting 'movements' and initiatives are where growth is to be found.

'One shall tell another, and he shall tell his friend, husbands, wives and children will come following in.'
(One shall tell another – Graham Kendrick)

Proclamation Evangelism

Preaching the gospel from the pulpit is the form of evangelism with which we are most familiar and comfortable. The power of God always

'How, then, can they call on the one they have not believed in? And how can they believe in the one of whom they have not heard? And how can they hear without someone preaching to them?' (Romans 10v 14)

accompanies the preaching of the gospel, and the preacher has a certain amount of liberty because people have 'chosen' to be there, even if chivvied along by friends or family. He will need his congregation to pray in support and help him follow up. Sometimes people are out the back door like a flash when the service finishes! Everyone has their part to play, we can all befriend and offer prayer.

Also, a service that isn't overtly evangelistic can bear a harvest. It's amazing how God can convict from passages that don't emphasize the gospel. The Holy Spirit is excellent at presenting people with a message that they think is personally crafted for them. It's extraordinary how God brings people along on a week when the message is so pertinent to them, and how the devil tries to keep them away. The pastor needs intercessors to be praying alongside the message in support. It's easier to follow up this kind of evangelism than mass evangelism, as there are smaller numbers and the pastoral ministry is at hand. God backs up His word, *'God also testified to it by signs, wonders and various miracles, and by gifts of the Holy Spirit distributed according to his will'.* (Hebrews 2v 4)

Creative Evangelism (drama, art, music, dance)

'Then the Lord said to Moses, "See, I have chosen Bezalel son of Uri, the son of Hur, of the tribe of Judah, and I have filled him with the Spirit of God, with wisdom, with understanding, with knowledge and with all kinds of skills—to make artistic designs for work in gold, silver and bronze, to cut and set stones, to work in wood, and to engage in all kinds of crafts.' (Ex 31v 1-5)

Craftsmen were the first people in the Bible we are told were anointed with the Holy Spirit. This method is obviously going to appeal to artistic people, although we can't always match the high standards in popular culture. It's quite normal now for there to be a prophetic artist at a conference painting alongside the worship and spoken ministry. While Christian art doesn't substitute the spoken gospel it can wonderfully enhance and invigorate the message.

I remember being so arrested by a picture of Christ in a church atrium (as if He was an industrial era miner); I sat down and studied it for a while before moving on. The arts can bypass 'strongholds' of the mind and speak spirit-to-spirit to the lost. Music can be extremely powerful in touching the heart, and there are 'Christian bands' in the contemporary music world, not always overt, but seeking to minister God's presence in what they do. Dance can be powerful at drawing a crowd and conveying emotion, we live in a visual age. There is a good deal of dancing in scripture.

Drama can present the gospel in non 'religious' ways, and people don't need to know they are watching a gospel presentation for it to be effective. The gospel is implicit in JRR Tolkien's *Lord of the Rings* and CS Lewis' *Narnia Chronicles*. Millions of people have heard the gospel, 'veiled' in these classic works, without explicitly knowing they were.

Public Transport Evangelism

This is not a universally recognised method but I have a friend who is called to London bus evangelism. I travelled with her from Greenwich peninsula as she took command of the top floor of the bus. She preached at the front, and did a great job, while I shrivelled up at the back. It was excruciating, even though nobody looked back at me. She continued fearlessly, despite continual verbal abuse, until finally we left the bus with a huge sigh of relief from me. Unlike me she kept her dignity throughout, no hasty departure. I took hours to unclench and repent for my cowardice!

This form of evangelism furnishes us with a captive audience; providing they take their ubiquitous earphones out, people must listen. The flip side of this coin is that it is a 'captive' audience. People with no choice can get angry, as we might if an atheist did the same. If we experiment in public transport evangelism we need to pray people aren't 'turned off' Jesus because we've misread the situation and He is guilty by association.

My approach is to pray when entering public transport, 'Lord here I am, I'm available to you if you need me to talk to anybody'. Sometimes, if I'm honest I'd rather not speak to anyone because I want to text my wife, but I try to offer God the time anyway. You might think, you're an evangelist, aren't you ready anyway? Well I'd like to think so, but Jesus is a gentleman, He loves a 'willing' servant. The results have been extraordinary. People have got up from where they were sitting a carriage further along to sit next to me. I've had some amazing chats about Jesus, some of which I will relay later in the book. Other times 'nothing' has happened, and I quietly prayed for the person sitting next to me, God may show me some area they need help with in their life. On occasion the carriage on a train, or cabin on a plane seems to fill up with the glory of God. We never know exactly what could happen...

'After they had gone a long time without food, Paul stood up before them and said: "Men, you should have taken my advice not to sail from Crete; then you would have spared yourselves this damage and loss. But now I urge you to keep up your courage, because not one of you will be lost; only the ship will be destroyed. Last night an angel of the God to whom I belong and whom I serve stood beside me and said, 'Do not be afraid, Paul. You must stand trial before Caesar; and God has graciously given you the lives of all who sail with you.' So keep up your courage, men, for I have faith in God that it will happen just as he told me. Nevertheless, we must run aground on some island."
(Acts 27v 21–26)

'The fruit of the righteous is a tree of life, and the one who is wise saves lives'. (Prov 11v 30)

Prophetic Evangelism

Using giftings in the prophetic to "speak" into particular situations, which we shall explore in more detail in Chapter 3. We can "picture" and summarize the relationship between prophetic evangelism and the more traditional forms of evangelism as indicated in Figure 1 below, where the "contact" points with the seeker can often be quite different. In this schematic, "PE" is of course Prophetic Evangelist.

Contact points

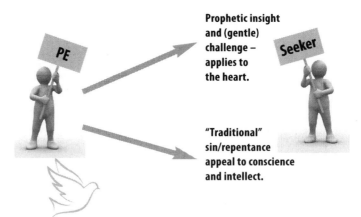

Fig 1

Part 2

The Prophetic through Scripture – when God speaks...

3 What is the prophetic?

Before diving headlong into the topic of the prophetic let us first look briefly at the nature of God. God is love, and love must be lavished on a subject in order to express itself. Love does not exist in a vacuum, by very nature it is active, looking for ways to express itself. God loves because He couldn't do otherwise, it would be against His nature. It is not a needy, self-orientated type of 'love' but selfless. Its reward is itself, love.

'In the beginning was the Word, and the Word was with God, and the Word was God'. (John 1v 1)

Orthodox Christianity is Trinitarian. God is three in one, one in three; Father, Son and Holy Spirit. God in Trinity is a relationship, this is one facet of God's nature. The love within the Trinity is boundless and self-giving. Father, Son and Spirit live to love and honour each other. Although a Trinity, yet they are One – truly this is a mystery. Love is creative and reproduces after its own likeness. Consider an expression of marital love; one result of consummated love is often reproduction, the miracle of a human baby who is made in the image of mother and father. Love relates, love communicates, love creates and love speaks.

What is prophecy?

The foundational truth undergirding prophecy is that God is love, and love always seeks to express and communicate itself. God is eternally communicating Himself and His invisible qualities through His Living Word, Jesus, His Holy Spirit, His creation and, last but not least, His people. It is unthinkable that we could say we love someone but never communicate with them. The result of love is that we share ourselves; our time, our thoughts, our energy and yes, our words. Love not expressed is love not received. Simply put the prophetic is hearing God and/or seeing what He is doing. Jesus modelled this beautifully to us as the scripture to the left demonstrates.

'I call on you, my God, for you will answer me;' (Psalm 17v 6a)

Hearing God is not some mysterious and difficult thing for a special and privileged breed of Christians, it is for all those who draw near to Him. God may not communicate to us all in exactly the same way, and we might not all hear with the same clarity, but He speaks nonetheless. After all we

'Jesus gave them this answer: "Very truly I tell you, the Son can do nothing by himself; he can do only what he sees his Father doing, because whatever the Father does the Son also does'.
(John 5v 19)

don't communicate with everyone we know in the same way. I love both my wife Bec and Anna my daughter very much, but the way I speak to them is naturally different. The prophetic is the ability to listen to what God is saying and communicating what we have heard out into the world. The office of the prophet is included in the ministry gifts (Eph 4) and prophecy is a spiritual gift (1 Corinthians 12v 8-10) as shown below.

Speaking Gifts	**Speaking in tongues**
	Interpretation of tongues
	Prophecy
Knowing Gifts	**Discerning of spirits**
	Word of knowledge
	Word of wisdom
Power Gifts	**Working of miracles**
	Faith
	Healing

The 'prophetic' is also an overarching term which deserves unpacking as it is essential to this book. *It is a general description which encompasses a clear word of prophecy from a prophet to all the speaking and knowing gifts above.* In Christian circles it is often used to describe someone who is recognisably 'spiritual' and more likely than most to say, 'could God be saying?' or 'we need to hear God first!'

We might not be a prophet; but all should have prophetic insight to a greater or lesser extent. We will discuss old and new testament 'prophets' in the next chapter but for now I emphasize we can all certainly hear God. A prophet is a person who hears or sees God's future (forth-telling) activity and passes it on in the written word and/or in speech. We all immediately think of Elijah and Jeremiah, Daniel and Moses, giants in their own right, but there is a huge spectrum of prophetic activity. Many Christians will be operating at a low level without knowing they are, even if their church doesn't teach such things overtly. In a general sense Christians who minister with either speaking or knowing gifts would be called prophetic. It's worth mentioning that the prophetic gifts can spark up the power gifts. So, for example, a word of knowledge to a stranger, *your right hip is in terrible pain and is crumbling*, releases huge faith in that person (whether or not they are Christian) and then when prayer for healing is received a miracle occurs.

I would like to share an example of how the prophetic can guide and comfort us, in this instance through a stressful transition. Hearing God does not mean that something will not be difficult. Actually, the fact that God is speaking directly might indicate that it will be tough, but it gives us the comfort of knowing He is with us in it.

We had moved from the rural 'idyll' of Hunstanton, Norfolk (where I had been pastoring) to the big bad city of London. I needed to spread my wings, Hunstanton is a tiny town which I felt had heard quite enough from me. I had been invited to be an itinerant for a year in a group of churches and the job came with accommodation in South London, otherwise there's no way we could have afforded to go. I leapt at the opportunity to be in a wider setting and for us all to explore the city. We arrived like Dick Whittington in August 2018. The year was going well, God gave us a lot of favour. We entertained hopes of being able to stay on and settle somehow, even though we had not been promised this. If this was of God, we decided, it would become possible somehow.

But after Christmas I was told definitively that there was no money and no job. I started frantically applying for jobs, every day at least once I searched the Christian job sites. But the gestation for an application is four to six months, not weeks, and jobs were few. With seven weeks to go I still had no definite offer of a job, no home for us to live in (wherever we were going!). We had no financial buffer, a year of living in South London had seen to that. Our options as a little family were running out, the wheels turning excruciatingly slowly on the six jobs I'd applied for. The days were ticking by, we had to vacate our cottage by August 2019. They had been so kind to us but they couldn't house us forever. It felt like Bec and I were aging a year for every week towards our deadline. We had no reason now to be anywhere except for my work and the call of God. We were renting out our property in Hunstanton which was the only thing that was keeping us financially afloat.

It was a strange feeling, like looking over the edge of the Grand Canyon at a vertiginous drop while my stomach turned somersaults. The world was our oyster, but it felt more like a black hole threatening to swallow us up. But God had not cut us adrift. He had been speaking to me about my work and family regularly over the last seven months, saying the same thing in several different ways. This is one of the prophetic pictures which strengthened me through this testing time:

We as a family stood at the end of a long jetty; I knew that we had to leave the jetty, but we could not turn around and come inland again. All our belongings were piled up beside us. There was nowhere else for us to advance, only a vast expanse of water as far as the eye could see. I didn't know if it was a huge lake like in the Rockies, or the sea. We were just like the Israelites leaving Egypt and arriving at the shores of the Red Sea. We could not go back nor could we stay where we were; we had to go forward but how? In our case the charioteers of Egypt were not racing up behind us to kill or capture us, even if it felt like it occasionally. Would God part the waters one more time just for us?

I started to weep; my personal disappointments weighed heavily, but I also felt the responsibility of my situation. I have failed my family, I have not provided for them, what are we going to do? There were no boats on the water, there was no apparent help for us to cross the water. Nothing was happening at all, the water was becalmed. The stillness of the water mocked the raging storm in my heart.

Then at seemingly the last minute a huge and beautiful eagle swooped down from above and behind and picked us all up on its broad back, along with our possessions. Then it effortlessly soared carrying us high over the waters and finally swooped down to deposit us in what I knew somehow to be a land of exquisite beauty and peace. I did not know whether this was a spiritual or natural beauty, or both.

This picture does not need expert interpretation, God is the eagle, just as He's described carrying the Israelites across the wilderness (Ex 19). This picture exactly described our situation and our feelings at that time. The job I wanted most of all those I'd applied for was the evangelist role at Through Faith Missions (TFM). It sounded brilliant, but the interview was not until the first week of July. I was juggling four to five different interviews, and opportunities to preach with a view. It was a waiting game; waiting, waiting, waiting. Everything depended on other people's timing. They didn't know that with every day the pressure ramped up on us. We held on to the words from God by our fingernails, barely keeping a lid on the rising panic.

My phone buzzed. I had travelled up to Coton, Cambridgeshire to interview for TFM at their office in the morning, and on the journey back to London my phone had died. As it charged up I could see I had a missed call. With bated breath I called and Paul Preston the Chair of trustees answered. They wanted me! Hallelujah. But we had to wait another week for the references to come through before we could finally celebrate. That week felt like another year.

Fast forward six weeks after trips back and forth to the Cambridgeshire area (The TFM office was in Coton). After three weeks with no fixed abode, and some other complications, we arrived in the height of summer to the picturesque town of St Ives. We were welcomed by neighbours, found the right local church the first Sunday and fell in love with the famous river, water meadows and the historic bridge. St Ives is definitely beautiful.

It was an incredible feeling to know that we had pinned everything on hearing from God and (after times in the past of getting it wrong) we had it exactly right. Our faith levels hit the ceiling. Phew, we had flown by the seat of our pants, the eagle had carried us and we were re-united with all of our possessions which had been in storage. Like Peter we had walked on the water, the living word of God, by faith, and made it to Jesus! Exhilarating! If we want to have stunning testimonies, we have to embrace certain 'tests'. We suggest seven:

Who does it?

Peter's fabulous sermon on the day of Pentecost includes the quote (left) from Joel. That Peter uses it in this way is a statement; *this is fulfilled in your hearing, the last days are starting now.* It's an inclusive promise, no one is left out. Not everyone will have the office of prophet and not all will be leaders, but nonetheless, all can prophesy. Prophetic pictures aren't reserved for full time evangelists, God wants us all to live by His word.

'In the last days, God says, I will pour out My Sprit on all people; your sons and daughters will prophesy, your young men will see visions, your old men will dream dreams. Even on my menservants and maidservants I will pour out My Spirit in those days, and they will prophesy... (Acts 2 v 17–18)

This is where we trip up, it's not an all or nothing scenario. We might not be the big prophet coming to town to confront the king and work miracles. Still we can in less ostentatious ways be prophetic in daily life. It's simply not biblical to narrow this ministry down to the exclusion of all but a very few people. You may not be an evangelist but that does not mean you can't evangelise. In fact it's the function of the evangelist to equip you for this. We do absolutely need leaders and teachers, but ones that want to empower us.

The inherent danger with an 'expert minister' dynamic is that he may not want to be 'trumped'. He may control the use of prophecy because he has grown to like being the man of power for the hour. We can think revival is the answer to all our problems, but if we get revival it will expose all the control bases and ambitions of those who are used to power. Think of how rattled the Pharisees were by the appearance of Jesus, and how quickly in their case jealousy degrades into murderous intent.

What Joel is describing is revival, when the word and Spirit of God are easily found, even those not actively looking will be overtaken by revelation and spiritual experiences. We have all heard about the amazing occurrences in the Welsh revival where people would fall on their knees in the street, nowhere near a church and repent, or in the Middle East currently where many Muslims are having dreams and visions of Jesus.

God's Spirit will not be controlled by us and we don't want to miss our visitation (Luke 19v 44) because He isn't doing things in the way we think He should. In the book of Numbers we get an insight into the humility and servant heart of Moses. Joshua is concerned because those absent at the impartation meeting where Moses shares his anointing, start to prophecy anyway. The challenge facing us in the world today is so vast, we needn't clutch prophecy to ourselves, there's room for all to hear God. This is Moses' response; and what a lovely insight into the heart of God.

'But Moses replied, "Are you jealous for my sake? I wish that all the LORD's people were prophets and that the LORD would put his Spirit on them!"
(Numbers 11v 9)

How do we know we're receiving?

'As he spoke, the Spirit came into me and raised me to my feet, and I heard him speaking to me'.
(Ezekiel 2v 2)

Later in the book we will examine this important subject in greater depth but for now we note that revelation from God often comes with a surge of hope and faith. Our story about how we finally arrived in St Ives was not by any means a stress free one. Every time God spoke to me there was a layer of peace and faith that came. There's a peace that we didn't have before. If we've been praying about a situation we may now feel free to move on to other things, we've prayed through.

'Receiving' from God is a very personal thing, but we may well feel a certainty and a solidity about something we have never had before. We doubt our doubts and believe our beliefs. There will be unique ways we hear, we all have our own relationship with Father God. We will start to recognise how He speaks to us and grow in confidence. Sometimes we need pastoral help, it was Eli who finally realised God was calling Samuel, not him. He told Samuel to go back and next time to say, *'speak Lord, your servant is listening'* (1 Samuel 3v 10).

When do we prophesy?

It may be that we are more likely to prophesy in a meeting with other believers because the presence of God is given in a corporate way, but circumstances do, of course, vary. The use of tongues can be very effective in stirring up other gifts, including prophecy. The Holy Spirit will guide us, especially as we exercise this gift. One thing is certain, prophecy is not meant to be restricted to when the people of God come together. There are times when the Holy Spirit will come upon us in a special way to prophesy, at other times it will be a still small voice in our spirits.

> *All the men of Judah, with their wives and children and little ones, stood there before the Lord. Then the Spirit of the Lord came on Jahaziel son of Zechariah, the son of Benaiah, the son of Jeiel, the son of Mattaniah, a Levite and descendant of Asaph, as he stood in the assembly.*
> *He said: "Listen, King Jehoshaphat and all who live in Judah and Jerusalem! This is what the Lord says to you: 'Do not be afraid or discouraged because of this vast army. For the battle is not yours, but God's.* (2 Chron 20v 13–15)

'Remember that people who prophesy are in control of their spirit and can take turns'. (1 Cor 14v 32 NLT)

Jumping up and down and insisting that we be allowed to speak immediately because 'God said' is not maturity. I've done it, and it's not something I'm proud of. It can be manipulative and off-putting; our attitude becomes the issue not the 'word'. Prophecy comes with an 'immediacy' and 'freshness' but that won't vanish if we have to wait politely ten minutes to share, or even tomorrow. We do it with wisdom. Later on we will look further at the importance of weighing a word; is this to share, is it to pray, is it to give to leadership or is it to simply wait and see if God confirms it?

How do we prophesy?

There are some general (character) principles of how we should prophesy. Suffice to say that the *gifts* of the Spirit sit best on the *fruit* of the Spirit. Later there will be more practical guidance. We are always aiming to build a relational bridge and share our message in such a way that it is most likely to be 'heard'.

Lovingly – If we share in love it is much more likely someone will 'hear' us. People can sense if we love them. Truth can be very stark if not couched in love, both are equally important. We all lean slightly towards love or truth because of our dispositions and experience, and it's good to be mindful of that as we prophesy. There are occult means of obtaining limited 'truth' but they always leave the person damaged and fearful. We want to bring people into the healing presence of Jesus. Without love it's all meaningless anyway. (1 Corinthians 13v 1)

Humbly – *'I think I'm right, but I could be wrong'*. We will investigate later in the book how New Testament prophecy differs from Old Testament. We do not generally prophesy in a didactic and confrontational way. We shouldn't model ourselves (only in passion for God) on some of the more eccentric Old Testament prophets unless God is specifically guiding us and showing our leaders likewise. We can be natural; no need to take the posture of Elijah confronting the prophets of Baal, or say 'thus saith the Lord'. King James English is not mandatory, or even necessary.

It's worth remembering that even if we are right in what we have heard, a person directly involved will not always tell us so. They may deny it outright. Our humility enables us to avoid a standoff, we can get badly off track if we need to be 'right'. If God gives us something to share with our home group and it is not taken up, He will show someone else as well. We don't need to manipulate things. A bad attitude can mean people 'miss' God in what we share. We can be confident and gentle at the same time. It is normally insecurity that causes people to be overbearing. God resists the proud (James 4v 6).

We can all 'hear' wrong and the danger is that we can cast our pearls before swine. We so want someone to 'get' what we are sensing in our Spirit that we unconsciously add to what God has said and take on the job of the Holy Spirit. It's His job to guide people into truth (John 16v 13)

Gently – There's no need for us to overstep our bounds, 'A gentle word can break a bone' (Proverbs 25v 15). A gentle 'word' can be powerful if we leave space for God to confirm it. This underrated fruit of the Spirit is very attractive especially to those who are used to being pushed around and controlled (Philippians 4 v5). God 'shouts' His truths and whispers His 'secrets'. 'LESS' really can be 'MORE!'

Generously – We have a generous God who sees the best in people. It's more blessed to give than receive. If we are not thanked or affirmed for what we share, it doesn't matter. We may be aware of obvious sin in someone's life, and so if God gives us a word that seems 'too generous' we can argue in our minds. Surely God couldn't speak such a great destiny over that person? God is the supreme psychologist, sometimes an affirmation and encouragement can break shame and addiction over someone as surely as a direct challenge. They already know what's 'wrong' with them. 'Zacchaeus, come down immediately. I must stay at your house today.' (Luke 19v 5)

The important thing is God notices our hearts and when we are seeking Him for others, He will often speak to us in unexpected ways. We'll never out-give God! (Luke 6v 38)

Why do we do it?

We prophesy because we love God and therefore love people. This world needs to hear the voice of its Maker and Redeemer. There's nothing more natural for us than to communicate with our Father and to hear what's on His heart. We are prophetic in our lifestyle because Jesus was the 'great prophet' (Deuteronomy 18v 15 and 18; Acts 3v 22–23) and in this as in every sense we long to follow in His footsteps and become like Him. More of this later ...

'But if I say, "I will not mention his word or speak anymore in his name," his word is in my heart like a fire, a fire shut up in my bones. I am weary of holding it in; indeed, I cannot'. (Jeremiah 20v 9)

Where do we do it?

Everywhere we can, appropriately. This gift is a blessing to the unbeliever as well as the saved. There is no situation where it can't work, so long as we are listening to God and available to Him.

'For the earth will be filled with the knowledge of the glory of the LORD as the waters cover the sea'. (Habbakuk 2v 14)

Prophecy – the real thing!

The real thing is fantastic, life-affirming, heart expanding, stronghold breaking, devil frightening, shame crushing and destiny calling!

'The LORD thundered from heaven; the voice of the Most High resounded'. (Psalm 18v 13)

I attended a small meeting called specially because a friend of ours Revd Bill Isaacs had some friends from Nigeria staying, one of whom was a blind prophet called Pious. I was happy just to observe, I wasn't in senior leadership at the time as this was ten years ago or more.

I thought I had been more or less unnoticed but at the end Pious said, before we go we must pray for Daniel. 'That's a great name for you', he started, 'the writing is on the wall for Daniel.' And proceeded to prophesy the most incredible words over me. Unfortunately, it was not recorded, and

I didn't remember everything because I was intent on receiving the impartation.

I had to be scraped off the floor sometime later. It felt something like how David must have marvelled after he had been called to his father's house and Samuel had poured the horn of oil over his head (1 Sam 16). He couldn't just go back to his sheep and sleep like any other night. Everything had changed, forever. Life would never be the same again.

For me not everything was different overnight, and the battle heated up, but that word is a personal anchor for me. There is not a shadow of doubt in my mind that Pious spoke to me the living word of God, and I would not trade it for anything. It was one of those 'Holy' moments that I'll remember for the rest of my life.

'We also have the prophetic message as something completely reliable, and you will do well to pay attention to it, as to a light shining in a dark place, until the day dawns and the morning star rises in your hearts'. (2 Peter 1v 19)

Appendix 6, page 169, helps to characterise prophecy in terms of its "macro" and "micro" applications.

4 Old and New Prophecy

'The nations you will dispossess listen to those who practise sorcery or divination. But as for you, the Lord your God has not permitted you to do so. The Lord your God will raise up for you a prophet like me from among you, from your fellow Israelites. You must listen to him. For this is what you asked of the Lord your God at Horeb on the day of the assembly when you said, "Let us not hear the voice of the Lord our God nor see this great fire anymore, or we will die."

The Lord said to me: "What they say is good. I will raise up for them a prophet like you from among their fellow Israelites, and I will put my words in his mouth. He will tell them everything I command him. I myself will call to account anyone who does not listen to my words that the prophet speaks in my name. But a prophet who presumes to speak in my name anything I have not commanded, or a prophet who speaks in the name of other gods, is to be put to death."

You may say to yourselves, "How can we know when a message has not been spoken by the Lord?" If what a prophet proclaims in the name of the Lord does not take place or come true, that is a message the Lord has not spoken. That prophet has spoken presumptuously, so do not be alarmed.
(Deut 18v 14-22)

God's plan is always to have a clear and anointed prophetic voice through which to challenge and teach His people. If God's people are obedient this communication would be unbroken, but because of their rebellion there is a historic breakdown in this flow. God gave them repeated warnings, but because of the hardness of their hearts Israel had no new revelation from God between the ministry of Malachi and John the Baptist. John burst onto the scene to preach repentance four hundred years after Malachi. This 'silence' from God in the 'intertestamental' period did mean that John's message, when it arrived, was even more dramatic and dynamic. Finally, God was speaking clearly again and commanding His rebellious people to repent.

'Jesus answered,
"My teaching is not my
own. It comes from the
one who sent me.'
(John 7v 16)

"I can see that you are a
prophet.' (John 4v 19b)

Is the prophetic for now?

Jesus is the pinnacle, the highest point of the prophetic ministry, the greatest prophet ever. He is the prophetic Everest that dwarfs the other peaks; Daniel, Jeremiah, Ezekiel, Isaiah and even Moses and Elijah. Jesus is mount Zion and Jerusalem surrounded by the other heights. He is the alpha and omega of the prophetic ministry. He is there with the Father and the Spirit as the world is created. He is there as the end times unfold prophetically in the book of Revelation. This book is saturated with Christ, it crams Jesus, the Lamb of God, into every cubic inch. Everything circles, gravitates towards and is tethered to Christ.

Jesus is, in a very real sense, the fulfilment and culmination of God's over-arching purposes revealed in the Old Testament. In saying this, we note of course that some elements of God's specific prophetic revelation still lie in the future. The gospels are brimming over with specific fulfilment of Messianic prophecy. Isaiah chapter 53 alone, is quoted or alluded to above eighty times in the new testament scriptures, underscoring its fulfillment in Christ. Jesus Himself makes it clear there is a prophetic step change as John the Baptist finishes his ministry of preparation, making 'straight the pathway' for Messiah Jesus (Matt 11v 11). From now on the least in the Kingdom of God is greater than the prophet John.

'For all the Prophets and the Law prophesied until John'. (Matt 11v 13)

'He said to them, "This is what I told you while I was still with you: Everything must be fulfilled that is written about me in the Law of Moses, the Prophets and the Psalms." (Luke 24v 44)

The purpose and intensity of this marvellous gift has changed slightly. It may be different in expression and function, but prophecy continues to sparkle and shine God's light into the church age. It is one of the gifts of Christ (often called ministry gifts) to His bride, His church.

So Christ himself gave the apostles, the prophets, the evangelists, the pastors and teachers, (Eph 4v 11)

Prophecy is included in all four lists of church gifts (Romans 12v 6-8, 1 Corinthians 12v 8-10, 1 Corinthians 12v 28-30 and of course Eph 4v 11). I have not found any scripture that suggests a rescinding of these gifts, quite the reverse. We walk steadily in the New Covenant in the full revelation of Christ, His Word and by His Spirit, but still we need the prod and encouragement of the prophetic gift. In our day prophecy is more of a fine tune, less a sledgehammer such as the ministry of Jeremiah or Elijah.

Do not treat prophecies with contempt,... (1 Thess 5v 19–20)

'for God's gifts and his call are irrevocable'. (Romans 11v 29)

Acts, the birth of the Church, is full of the prophetic gift. Prophecy drives forward the apostolic strategy and evangelism. It steers the fledgling church through all manner of challenges, through choppy waters full of perilous deceptions and towards mission fields ready for harvest. Prophecy pierces darkness, challenges falsehood, and corrects confusion. It was prophets and teachers who set aside Paul and Barnabas for their first missionary journey.

(NB. It is good practice for prophets to be around teachers and pastors; these complementary ministries are a mutual protection from excess and deception)

'While they were worshipping the Lord and fasting, the Holy Spirit said, "Set apart for me Barnabas and Saul for the work to which I have called them." (Acts 13v 2)

We are told Philip's four daughters could prophesy, and we are introduced to Agabus, the only person (excepting Judas and Silas in Acts 15) in the new church given the office of prophet, **'Leaving the next day, we reached Caesarea, and we went to stay at the home of Philip the evangelist, who was one of the Seven. After we had been there several days, a prophet named Agabus came down from Judea'.** (Acts 21 8–10)

Agabus famously warned Paul with prophetic action (ie. tying a belt around himself) what was awaiting him in Jerusalem. Paul prophesies to the soldiers and sailors on the ship sailing to Rome in Acts 27, before and during the ill-fated trip. In fact, it is not unreasonable to assume all the apostles could prophesy up to a point.

Paul's Corinthian letters teach the correct usage of prophesy, certainly not the abrogation of it. The prophetic is implicit, if not always explicit, in the other epistles and pastoral letters. Timothy's gift is widely considered to be a prophetic one, and Paul certainly did not want it shutting down; it was an important tool in church leadership.

'Follow the way of love and eagerly desire gifts of the Spirit, especially prophecy'. (1 Cor 14v 1)

'For this reason I remind you to fan into flame the gift of God, which is in you through the laying on of my hands'. (2 Tim 1v 6)

Revelation is entirely a prophetic book, the last in the Bible and the only one promising a blessing for reading it and a warning of judgement for anyone who takes away from it. John is fondly called the apostle of love.

He could equally be heralded one of the great New Testament prophets. John was eagle-eyed where it came to things of the Spirit. It is no coincidence that love and prophecy are conjoined in his ministry.

In chapter 11 we have the two witnesses, almost certainly representing the followers of the Lamb, they prophesy and give testimony. The prophecy is so fiery and their testimony so unyielding that it 'torments' the rebellious world which collectively refuses such a message.

Main differences between
Old and New Testament prophecy

The Old Testament has seventeen books of prophecy while the New Testament has one. This is a significant indication of how prophecy was needed to steer God's people towards, and prepare them for, the incarnation and ministry of Christ. The book of Revelation seems to concentrate on the future and the second coming of Christ (although there are multiple ways of interpreting it and some would disagree with me).

The Old Testament prophet often acted as the mouthpiece of God's direct and verbatim revelation to the Hebrew people of God, speaking forth His words verbatim. He was held accountable for his words (something we could learn from) by God's people. If prophecy did not come to pass he could be stoned at the city gates. Ironically, this didn't happen much to (false) prophets who got it wrong, but God's prophets were persecuted and killed in all sorts of horrible ways. They were correct in their message but it was rejected nonetheless. John the Baptist is a prime example of this (Matt 14v 1-13).

'But the prophet who prophesies peace will be recognized as one truly sent by the LORD only if his prediction comes true.' (Jer 28v 9) The prophet would operate independently and come to the king with direct revelation and instruction from God. This was often prophecy related to the actions or inactions of the governing authorities, and the prophet's courage was tested when they had to bring unwanted messages and bad news to Power. Often the prophet (ie. Samuel with Saul and David) would anoint the future King, thus affirming God's investment in the King as the instrument of His purposes. As in the case of Samuel, it could be a thankless task, *'Rejoice and be glad, because great is your reward in heaven, for in the same way they persecuted the prophets who were before you'*. (Matt 5v 12)

In the Old Testament, prophecy always glorified God and demonstrated His holiness as it pointed to the Messiah. There were many messages of judgement which were didactically delivered, and when God spoke through pictures and prophetic action His meaning was unmistakable.

The Old Testament prophecies looked forward as they spied on tiptoes the coming Messiah and Prophet. (2 Peter 1v19-21) They warned and cajoled God's people and called for obedience. God needed a set apart and Holy Nation (Deut 14v 2) into which to send His Son. Old Testament prophecy looks forward to Christ, New Testament prophecy flows out of Christ. We have our full truth in Him and His teachings, He is our meta-narrative.

When New Testament prophecy looks forward it is to the Tribulation and to the second coming of Christ. The incarnation, baptism, ministry, teaching, miracles, passion, death, burial, resurrection, ascension and outpouring of the Spirit have already happened. *'It is finished!'* New Testament prophecy speaks out of the revelation of Christ, it reaches back and brings forward the message of the Gospel, the Cross and the resurrection. Often it is not a 'new' word but an 'old' one brought forward into timely remembrance. It is 'supercharged' truth.

'For from him and through him and for him are all things. To him be the glory forever! Amen'. (Romans 11v 36)

In the Old Testament accuracy was presumed. The issue was would people respond with obedience or disobedience to the word of the Lord? 'See, I set before you today life and prosperity, death and destruction' (Deut 30v 15). Oftentimes the people were told clearly what would result from their response. There was no room for denial.

Today there is no assumption that God speaks directly to a nation as He did to ancient Israel, although many argue today God is still speaking to His people Israel. In writing this I am well aware of complexities and controversies surrounding this subject! These are controversies that defy easy or swift resolution. This subject requires a least a book in its own right to do it justice. Today we understand that the 'nation' through which God amplifies His prophetic messages is collectively the faithful and obedient people of God, (1 Peter 2v 9) whether Jew or Gentile (Gal 3v 28). The age old battle for God's people remains – to choose obedience not disobedience, life not death!

'But the one who prophesies speaks to people for their strengthening, encouraging and comfort'. (1 Corinthians 14v 3)

The relationship between prophecy in the biblical canon and today's prophetic evangelism

Biblical prophecy stands eternally – it is a fixed canon and recorded as such. Prophetic evangelism, by contrast, links the needs and exigencies of the present with the biblical pattern, showing all the characteristics of the biblical, yet applied directly to today's needs and challenges. Prophetic evangelism never contradicts Scripture. It is always in agreement with Scripture. This relationship is suggested schematically in Appendix 8.

What prophecy is not

Sometimes it's helpful in our learning and growing to understand what something is not, as we learn simultaneously what it is. These are two sides of the same 'prophetic' coin.

Our chance to promote our favourite doctrine or denominational emphasis

'For when one says, "I follow Paul," and another, "I follow Apollos," are you not mere human beings?' (1 Cor 3v 4)

Prophetic evangelism done well brings people into an awareness of the God Who knows them by name and cares about them passionately (Psalm 139). Leading people to the feet of Jesus is the focus, not educating someone on why the Baptists have got it right, or the Pentecostals etc. Someone on the street doesn't need these complexities, they're confused enough about Christianity already. Let's be careful we are not promoting a denomination or doctrine above Christ. 'I resolved to know nothing while I was with you except Christ Jesus, and Him crucified' (1 Cor 2v 2). Inculcating passion for Jesus is our aim. We don't gain anything by passing on our baggage, and nor do our listeners.

Our chance to look good

'Truly I tell you, they have received their reward in full'. (Matt 6v 2)

If we get a word of knowledge or some prophecy spot on, it's not so we can rest on our laurels. 'How anointed I am today, I can't wait to tell my friends!' Quite the reverse, we have gained a ten second window to talk to someone and now the hard work starts; let's not waste our 'gospel' window. God will know our 'worth' even if others never find out.

Our chance to feel good

'An argument started among the disciples as to which of them would be the greatest'. (Luke 9v 46)

It's nice if people prophesy pleasant things over us and recognise qualities that we feel are overdue a mention. This can become incestuous and inward looking if we are not careful. We can start comparing our 'word' with someone else's in an unhelpful way. God is working in different ways and at different speeds in all of us so what He speaks to us publicly is only a glimpse at the overall picture.

The great thing about prophetic evangelism is that it directs prophecy outwards towards the lost. The focus is in the right place, for the sake of the lost. The Holy Spirit is delighted when we use His gifts in this way. When we reach the lost God blesses us anyway.

'But seek first his kingdom and his righteousness, and all these things will be given to you as well'. (Matt 6 v33)

Our chance to get one over the pastor

Maybe we feel slapped down by the pastor and we think he's totally wrong. Prophesying along these lines on the Sunday morning in front of the church is not the way to go. Pastors will know the kind of games that can go on. Someone can be 'right' in their gift but 'wrong' in the way they handle it.

Sometimes I've sat in prayer meetings, particularly in joint ones, and wished that 'brother Matt or sister Marg' would decide whether they are praying to God or teaching the rest of us. Perhaps we've all done this occasionally, but we need to decide who we're communicating with. Prophecy is not our opportunity to inform others what they really should think, and if we misuse prophecy people won't listen when we're 'hitting the bullseye'.

> *"You have gone too far! The whole community of Israel has been set apart by the LORD, and he is with all of us. What right do you have to act as though you are greater than the rest of the LORD's people?"*
> (Numbers 16 v 3 NLT)

Our chance to co-opt God into our agenda

It's exasperating when Christians preface everything, even small decisions, with 'God told me' or 'God said'. This defensive stance rules out any dialogue or accountability about what might not actually be from God. We're manipulated into agreeing, or we are 'contradicting' God. Prophecy is not a spiritual weapon to bulldoze through something that would be resisted in any other context.

As a pastor I had a wry smile when people phoned or texted me to assert 'God has told me not to come to the prayer meeting for a month'. I scratched my head, 'would God really say that?' Maybe, but it's just an example of how tempting it is to shield ourselves behind 'God said'.

Let's reserve 'God said' to the rarest occasion when we are certain.

> *'Now when Joshua was near Jericho, he looked up and saw a man standing in front of him with a drawn sword in His hand. Joshua approached Him and asked, "Are You for us or for our enemies?"*
> (Joshua 5 v 13–14)

Where God's Logos word is concerned the more we memorise it and speak it as led by the Spirit the better, no danger there. I had a friend who could prophesy with scripture, he knew chunks by heart. He beautifully evoked gospel stories as he prophesied. God's Word is powerful and dynamically alive, to the extent we know it intimately, we'll find the Spirit of God draws it out of us as and when we prophesy.

'Open wide your mouth and I will fill it'. (Psalm 82v 10b)

In this chapter we have explored in outline what 'old' and 'new' prophecy is – and some of the things it is not. In the next chapter we turn our attention to false prophecy.

5 False Prophecy – Occult influences

'When you enter the land the Lord your God is giving you, do not learn to imitate the detestable ways of the nations there. Let no one be found among you who sacrifices their son or daughter in the fire, who practises divination or sorcery, interprets omens, engages in witchcraft, or casts spells, or who is a medium or spiritist or who consults the dead. Anyone who does these things is detestable to the Lord; because of these same detestable practices the Lord your God will drive out those nations before you. You must be blameless before the Lord your God'. (Deut 18v 9–13)

Whatever is good and given by God for edification will always precipitate a counterfeit by satan, attempting to cause damage and lead people astray. There are a plethora of occult means of 'prophecy'; divination, seances, tarot readings, fortune telling, runes, and ouija boards to name a few. While there is a certain level of 'information' that can be gathered; ultimately it is fake– a bit like the modern problem of 'fake news'! In the process the devil binds people up into sickness, mental illness, disease, dependency and demonization.

These methods are to be absolutely shunned, hence God's stern and repeated warnings throughout scripture. This way leads to destruction, torment, darkness and even suicide. There is no mercy in the demonic kingdom, and if the devil gets a toehold into someone's life he exerts a heavy price. He presses home his advantage to kill, steal and destroy all he can (John 10v 10a). I've seen enough (demonic) deliverance to know this darkness is real and personal. There is always a way back with God but best not to need it in the first place.

We need to be aware that even in 'secular' philosophies, at the centre and in the core leadership there is often a huge amount of occult activity. Nazism for example was an occult movement. Today Politicians of all varieties, even professing 'atheists' have occult advisors. Desperate people in need will seek 'extra' help from the occult and sometimes also from Christian prophecy. Look at the Old Testament accounts of Joseph and

Daniel, in the court of their kings they were surrounded and opposed by occult magicians and the battle raged as to whose 'revelation' would be trusted. Normally there was a point when the King realised that the occult counsellors were telling him what he wanted to hear, but those who had the Spirit of God spoke truth. Moses was in contest with the magicians of Pharaoh's court but there came a point where their 'signs' could go no further (Ex 8v 18). There is nothing new under the sun; our battle is spiritual. To the victor goes the spoils.

If we are going to walk closely with God, and especially if we want to function in prophetic gifts, it is essential that we repent for occult activity. This remains true even if we engaged in ignorance with our friends who thought it was just a bit of fun. It is not to them we will have to give an account of our lives, and we can't blame others for our decisions,

'Now the Spirit expressly states that in later times some will abandon the faith to follow deceitful spirits and the teachings of demons' (1 Tim 4v 1)

Beware false prophecy

'For false Messiahs and false prophets will appear; they will perform great miracles and wonders in order to deceive even God's chosen people, if possible'.
(Matt 24v 24)

When I was at high school there was a craze for 'automatic writing'. This is where a passive human hand holding a pen starts to write a 'spirit' message, everyone was trying it and it works! It took off like a house on fire, and was causing such disruption that there was a special assembly to address it. Our deputy head who was in his own words, not a Christian or a spiritual person, condemned it as 'evil'.

Witchcraft is mainstream in our society now and unashamedly flaunts itself. It is so pervasive we might accept as normal something that is actually occult. If we repent for engaging in any of these activities, we can be cleansed and enjoy hearing from our loving heavenly Father. What starts out as something that's a giggle and a bit fringy can quickly degrade into bondage. The great news is that even if we have stepped into something dark, either in ignorance or in deliberate rebellion, Jesus is expert at untying us,

'The reason the Son of God appeared was to destroy the devil's work'.
(1 John 3v 8b)

Getting free

'So if the Son sets you free, you will be free indeed'.
(John 8v 36)

We need to repent and get ourselves washed from any spiritual darkness, there's no shame in this. Repentance is a wonderful gift. I've not met any Christian who didn't need some level of spiritual cleansing. We might need some deliverance and pastoral support to appropriate freedom, depending on how deeply we were involved. The Holy Spirit will guide us to get rid of occult objects in our homes, yes, even if they were gifted by a beloved family member. We might need a bonfire - as in the book of Acts (19v 19).

There is a simple procedure, easy to remember, that can help us get free. It works for occult involvement (as every area of sin), I have included some hypothetical examples.

Recognise – I do have some borderline occult books that I feel uncomfortable about. The more I think about them, I feel cold inside. It's time for them to go to the incinerator!

Repent – I'm turning away from my morning astrology chart and depending on Jesus; He's the only one who can tell me about my day! I'm not blaming the person who got me into it and told me it was fine; this is my sin and I own it. Please forgive me Jesus, my Creator and Redeemer, for going to another source for comfort and guidance. Be my guide and counsellor, and no-other, from this day forward.

Renounce – I utterly renounce the words that the gypsy spoke over me, and I break their power over me in Jesus' name. I am a child of God and only my heavenly Father gets to tell me who I am.

Resist – NO, satan, you have been driven out in Jesus' name and cannot come back. This house is swept clean and filled with the Holy Spirit (Matt 12v 43). I'm filling my mind with the light of God's word and enjoying communion with Jesus. Nothing will tempt me back to that darkness. As we do this God will wash us clean, and if there's a contesting we will prevail,

'If we confess our sins, he is faithful and just and will forgive us our sins and purify us from all unrighteousness' (1 John 1v 9).

If we have a developing spiritual gifting God will redeem our past experiences and, in time, use them for His glory. Then we may proceed without any concern that we might bring an impure flow, tinged with past non-Christian spirituality. Even as believers we note that as and when we lay hands on people in Ministry, it is possible for them to receive from us spiritually both good and bad, simultaneously. That is why it is vital for the Christian Minister (prophetic evangelist) to submit past experiences to Jesus so they be completely sanctified for His service.

Those that have a spiritual 'antennae' such as being 'psychic', (maybe a 'gift' passed down from a parent), when cleansed are often gifted prophetically. God never takes something away without replacing it with something beautiful, and better! He gives us beauty for ashes.

A good friend of ours who is Cherokee Indian by birth used to have all manner of occult dreams and experiences from her Indian heritage and ancestor worship, but has now been cleansed by the blood of Jesus. It was a serious fight to get free but she is now wonderfully blessed in Holy Spirit dreams and regularly wakes up singing worship songs at night. She brings the redemptive strengths of her heritage into the kingdom of God with none of the darkness. Thank you Jesus.

We must take occult activity seriously, and be ruthlessly honest with ourselves, without fear. We cannot mess around in the enemy kingdom and expect to come away unscathed. It's possible to have a 'mixed' gift; i.e. part psychic gift and part prophetic gift. It is a horrible and unsettling experience to hear someone operate like this even if they are 'right' in what they are saying. In Acts the apostolic team are in Philippi, and as they go to the place of prayer there is a girl with a spirit of divination following Paul and Barnabas around shouting, *"These men are servants of the Most High God, who are proclaiming to you the way of salvation."* (Acts 16v 17)

She was speaking 'truth' but it was aggravating Paul until finally he cast the divining spirit out of her. Just because someone says the right thing doesn't mean they are of the right spirit. There are many spirits that have gone out into the world, not all spirituality is synonymous with Holy Spirit activity (1 John 4v 1). We must pay attention to the Holy Spirit in us Who will warn us if something isn't right. If we are willing to submit to one-another in love, we mustn't mind someone who can discern spirits pointing out that we need cleansing. In fact, it is wisdom to invite accountability. If they are wrong, we've lost nothing, except maybe some pride that needed to go anyway!

We need to seek balance in all things. The purpose of looking briefly at false prophecy is not to paralyse us with fear of causing damage. If we wait until we're mature in every way before we try to prophesy, we'll never do it. That's not our aim at all, quite the reverse. The antidote to false prophecy, and incorrect use of the prophetic gift, is not to shut down on it completely. Sadly, so many churches do this, and pay the price for it. *'Do not quench the spirit. Do not treat prophecies with contempt'* (1 Thess 5v 19a). The correct use of the gift undergirded by sound teaching is the solution. We must believe that God's ability to guide us is greater than the devil's cunning to deceive us. Anything worth having in the Kingdom of God costs us something to step into, even when it is free! This is a vast subject; suffice to say it one of many (apparent) Kingdom paradoxes!

We must be convinced that God loves us, is speaking to us and will meet us as we step out in faith. The simple fact that you are reading this shows that your heart is already in the right place, you want to be right with God. Sometimes keen people get wrongly convicted, or should I say condemned, because they earnestly want transparency with God! Procrastination, as we know, is the thief of time, and time is short. Introspection is a similar trap. Perhaps therefore Paul reminded Timothy, who many commentators think had a gift of prophecy,

'For this reason I remind you to fan into flame the gift of God, which is in you through the laying on of my hands.' (2 Timothy 1v 6)

What about the mis-use or abuse of prophecy I have seen?

I attended a joint church service many years ago. In the ministry time at the end a lady started to prophesy over me. I was blessed to begin with, the message was right, but as she carried on something changed and it turned sour. There was a horrible driven edge to what she was saying, 'You must study the Bible, study the bible, study the bible'. I felt sick inside, (this is something I experience, spiritually, when something is 'off') but she proceeded oblivious to my distress. You might think, how could it be wrong to encourage someone to study the bible? There was a tangible spiritual pressure to what she said, maybe something that God needed to deal with in her, that oppressed my spirit. I love to study the bible, I was already doing that and didn't need to be rebuked or cajoled to do it.

If I had my time again I would have stopped her. It's always easier after the event to decide what we should have done! She meant well but should have stopped 'prophesying' long before she did. Hindsight is twenty twenty! Others commented that the prophecy wasn't right and I felt sick for a whole day. Only after repeated prayer forgiving the lady, was the impact of those words broken, the pressure lifted and my peace slowly returned. It was not an experience I want to repeat, and I certainly never want to do that to anyone else.

The lady may never have known how destructive her words were, and I would hesitate to say they came from an evil spirit. Possibly they originated from her spirit not the Holy Spirit. We live and learn. But imagine how counter-productive it would be for a non-Christian to experience anything like this before they've heard about Jesus or made up their mind about him, it's unthinkable.

'Do not be quick with your mouth, do not be hasty in your heart to utter

anything before God. God is in heaven and you are on earth, so let your words be few'. (Ecclesiastes 5v 2)

We are responsible for our decisions

Just because someone can prophesy doesn't mean they are close to God. When He generously gives good gifts God does not snatch them back if they are taken for granted or used independently of Him (Romans 11v 29). After all Caiaphas the high priest, who was far away from God in his heart could still prophesy accurately, 'You do not realize that it is better for you that one man die for the people than that the whole nation perish." (John 11v 50). Or in one the most sobering verses in the Bible, *'Many will say to me on that day, 'Lord, Lord, did we not prophesy in your name and in your name drive out demons and in your name perform many miracles?' Then I will tell them plainly, 'I never knew you. Away from me, you evildoers!'* (Matt 7v 22–23)

Returning to my negative experience, afterwards I had a choice, do I shut down on the prophetic altogether? I have met people who are hurting after a bad experience. Maybe they felt exposed in the way personal prophecy was delivered (i.e. in front of their whole church) or something was spoken over them that was false. And now they don't want anything to do with the prophetic.

In my discipleship training small group, during the first week when everything was new and vulnerable, somebody prophesied over me a word which was false, and the opposite of what I was doing. Even if it was right, which it wasn't, it would have been bad practice, but he was senior to me and I didn't have the courage to challenge him outright. I was impotently furious with him. I felt really exposed, and it took months for me to properly forgive him and begin to trust again. I've noticed that if our gifting and destiny lie in a specific ministry area the devil will work overtime to contaminate our experience and make us turn our back on it.

The bad experience is evidence that there can be a good, even great experience. We can be cleansed and healed from the former and learn tremendously from it, it's all spiritual 'grist for the mill'! When I prophesy over people I am aware of not reproducing that which was negative for me, it puts a healthy restraint on my enthusiasm. We're all on a learning curve and we need to recognise the human element. Immaturity is not impurity. We do the best we can with what we've got.

Not everyone has been taught, or taught well, how to handle the prophetic, but God's grace is available to everyone! (James 4v 6). If we're humble and honest enough we can learn and grow together. We must choose to forgive those that have unwittingly damaged us, ask God to cleanse us and step forward in faith. It bears repeating, the antidote to incorrect use of the prophetic is not 'intertestamental silence' but correct and Christ-centric prophecy.

'But we do not belong to those who shrink back and are destroyed, but to those who have faith and are saved'. (Hebrews 10v 39)

Readers may want to refer at this point to Appendix 10 – False Teaching on the Prophetic.

6 How do I know I'm hearing God?

Imagine for a minute a Galilean shepherd at a large watering hole. There are thousands of sheep jostling to get to the drinking water and many shepherds milling around. The sheep all look the same. No-one could separate them effectively, it's chaotic. This is until one shepherd gets up from his lunch and whistles as he walks away without turning around. One hundred and forty five sheep wiggle through and jump over the massed flocks following him into the desert. They would not be led by anyone else. They recognise his voice above all the commotion and noise, this is their shepherd, they respond instinctively to his voice.

'My sheep listen to my voice; I know them, and they follow me'.
(John 10v 27)

Where revelation is concerned there are four voices we can hear, the one we want to follow is our 'good shepherd.' We will learn to distinguish between them later.

- **God's (the shepherd's) voice**
- **Our heart**
- **The enemy**
- **Other people's hearts**

On the next page, we're going to outline some general principles for receiving revelation. I want you to imagine each one of these 'sails' is on a ship in a fleet sailing to a God-given destination on a God-given assignment. If they are all separated and even crashing into to each other we conclude, this is not revelation from God, (Fig 2 overleaf) and now is not the time to make 'life' decisions!

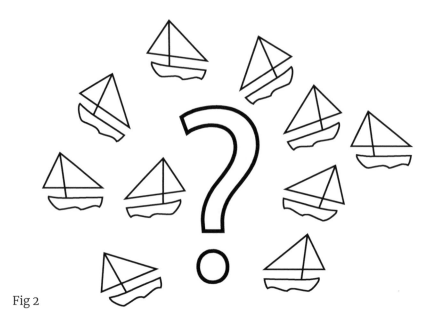

Fig 2

If we've heard clearly from God, the ships in the fleet (Figure 3 below) should be pointing in roughly the same direction; the wind blowing them towards the same place. Our God is a God of order. Occasionally one or two might be at right angles or tacking but on the whole they are pleasingly symmetrical.

We must settle in our own hearts that God's commitment to lead us is much stronger than the devil's determination to deceive us. If we want to be led, God will lead us! These pointers represent the sails on the ships.

Fig 3

TEN POINTERS/SAILS

These would tend to be for big decisions like moving house, changing job or getting married. The principles, however, hold true and are good pointers in all of life and ministry. If we have them in the back of our minds they will inform how we process revelation.

1. Does it line up with God's word?

God will never contradict Himself and so we must thoroughly acquaint ourselves in His Word. His moral will is perfectly clear and unlike humans He doesn't do unexpected U-turns. Someone says, 'God's told me to leave my wife and kids, forget my mortgage and go and serve him in Pakistan with a local bride'. We can categorically say this is not a message from God, it cuts right across His Word. You might think this scenario is far-fetched, it isn't. There is all sorts of weird stuff out there masquerading as the prophetic. We are told to test the fruit, in this case of prophetic words, *'By their fruit you will recognize them. Do people pick grapes from thorn bushes, or figs from thistles'* (Matt 7v 16)

> *God is not human, that he should lie, not a human being, that he should change his mind. Does he speak and then not act? Does he promise and not fulfil?'* (Numbers 23v 19)

The Word of God is our plumb line and the first place we should test guidance; if it doesn't pass this test then we can stop here. Although we are all special in God's eyes, He doesn't have 'special' arrangements with individuals where His standards are lowered. If God is telling us to mow our neighbour's lawn, and our neighbour happens to be an elderly widow, and send a thousand pounds to an orphanage in Sudan, this falls clearly into the scriptural pattern of God's concern for widows and orphans. (James 1v 27) Common sense in applying God's Word can get us a long way.

The more of God's Word we hide in our hearts and store in our minds, the easier it is for God to guide us. His will is contained in His Living Word. His Word is in full and beautiful congruence with His Spirit; they will never contradict, only complement and confirm each other. If we want to flow in the Spirit, we must live in the Word of God.

> *Keep this Book of the Law always on your lips; meditate on it day and night, so that you may be careful to do everything written in it. Then you will be prosperous and successful.* (Josh 1v 8)

2. Is it in the general flow of what God has been doing in our life?

Some of us have followed Jesus for some time and it has dawned on us that He's been slowly chipping away at the rock in our lives to reveal Michelangelo's 'David'. Our calling, gifts and sanctified passions are

"Before I formed you in the womb I knew you, before you were born I set you apart; I appointed you as a prophet to the nations."
(Jer 1v 5)

chiselled to become ever sharper and lines clearer. There are prophecies that have been given to us by too many different people for it to be a coincidence. There are desires in our hearts that won't go away and they stir our passion every time we think of them.

There's a process of spiritual osmosis over time so that what's in God's heart fills our heart and vice versa. There are exciting moments along the way when we leap forward into our calling, but then we're back in God's workshop being refined. The ships are starting to line up.

In the extraordinary case of the apostle Paul, his life has a dramatic turn around but with hindsight his calling seems so obvious. He's passionate, sold out, extremely well versed in the Scriptures and one of the best theological minds in world history. It's largely from Paul's epistles that we get our Salvation doctrine, church theology and teaching on living out our faith. Paul's epistles are a catalyst of the teaching of Jesus, bringing it all together in the context of a mission field that is 'going global.'

In one sense Paul's transformation is dramatic but in hindsight, he is the perfect person for his calling. Where guidance is concerned we can take the long view and say, this isn't a 'fly by night' change, it's been a long time coming. Or no, it just doesn't fit with all the other things God's been doing in me. If we've had a heart to serve in China for years, and then suddenly we feel called to Germany, either this is a red herring and a distraction, or we need to investigate. Maybe there's an ex-pat Chinese community in Berlin that needs a missionary?

3. Do the trusted people God has put around us witness that this is of God?

'Plans fail for lack of counsel, but with many advisers they succeed'.
(Provv 15v 22)

God has put us in Church and under Godly leadership for many reasons including our own personal good. We do not have to submit when the pastor or leader is saying what we want to hear. Submission is only proved when our leader puts the brakes on or even stops us temporarily. There's a safety in sharing our plans and a Godly order in allowing leaders to weigh our 'revelation.' We have to be humble enough to admit that we don't see the whole picture. This pre-supposes that our leaders are Godly and in the flow of the Spirit. Even if they are not, however, God is still able to work His purposes through them. Eli for instance, had serious flaws as a father and priest but could still spot the anointing on Samuel (1 Samuel) and helped him to follow it. It is Eli who discerns that God is calling Samuel and advises him to say

'Speak Lord your servant is listening' (1 Sam 3v 1-10).

Before we reach maturity our parents have authority and responsibility for us (and we respect them all our lives Eph 6v 2). They have experienced more of the world than we, and they know us better than anyone. Even if they are not Christians, if we submit to their authority God then will work through that. If we are required to wait because they don't give permission at once, this will work the grace of God into us, and our call will be stronger for being tested. The authority figures in our lives can help us find the wisdom of God, imperfect as they may be. Jethro helps Moses to see he needs to delegate a job that is crushing him (Ex 18v 18).

In Antioch we're told that the teachers and prophets set Paul and Barnabas aside. It wasn't Paul's suggestion, at least we're not told that Paul submitted to the leadership team. The irony is that if God is calling us to do something which we try to facilitate with our own strength then we might have to wait longer. Infamously Abraham and Sarah thought they would give God a helping hand in providing an heir (Gen 16v 1-2). Hagar produced Ishmael, and there has been trouble ever since between the descendants of Isaac (who came much later) and Ishmael. The prophetic tends to get more specific according to the difficulty of the assignment being given. King Saul for example had some incredibly accurate prophetic details given to him as he was called to be King (1 Sam 10v 1-16).

4. Is there a mixture of revelation, Spirit and flesh?

It would be foolish to think that we don't bring some personal agendas with us into our serving of God. For example if I felt called to serve the Lord in the sunny climbs of Crete, an island I love, it might be hard for me to be objective. If our passion for the lost can't be quenched then the enemy is very invested in slipping in some false revelation. He wants to push us too fast into something before we are ready, or our mission field is prepared by God. God's timing is perfect. We must trust that even if from our perspective things look very messy. There is a presumption that doesn't please God. (Psalm 19v 12)

There can be a danger that we receive a calling from the Spirit and proceed to chase it with the 'flesh' (Gal 3v 3). Once I tried to help God ease me into the next phase of my ministry. I offered to help at a parachurch organisation as I loved the people there. I was also keen that my 'call' could be spotted and harboured hopes that ministry opportunities might open up for me. Just in case God had forgotten! I peeled vegetables in a kitchen for eight months, made pots of tea for the team and drove to and from the rail station to pick up visiting speakers. All very worthy service, no shame in that. However, there must have been the constant smell of burning flesh coming through the kitchen hatch (my flesh)!

I watched people ten years younger than me get the opportunities I desperately wanted and thought I deserved. While visiting students were in small groups, I wrote out endless library cards by hand. At the end of my time there I learned that the library system would be computerised after all. Hundreds of handwritten cards were thrown in the recycling, I felt like 'Private Benjamin' at boot camp painting tonnes of coal white.

God used that experience and redeemed it, but I had a good object lesson in learning to let God do the promoting in His Own timing (Psalm 76v 6-7). Sometimes God may allow leaders to overlook or misunderstand us because it purifies the call on our lives. God is carefully watching our reactions. An occasional 'Saul' might even throw a (metaphorical) spear at us (1 Sam 19v 10). We need to know where our real security lies, in God and His destiny for our lives and not in the fluid opinions of man. We can't be separated from our destiny. No man, demon or angel can knock us off course while we keep following Jesus (Romans 8v 38).

5. Have we been prepared/trained for this?

'The horse is made ready for the day of battle, but victory rests with the LORD'. (Prov 21v 31) There are many ways that God trains us, formally (through Bible college, discipleship etc.) and informally. There's the university of life, experiences both good and bad and mentors who spiritually input our lives and guide us. There is our gift-mix and overall calling to consider as well. Obviously we can have ups and downs in the Christian walk but when we look back we can discern a definite pattern and direction. The apostles had extreme highs and lows but as they reflected on their days with Jesus they knew how expertly they had been prepared and positioned for the outpouring of the Holy Spirit at Pentecost.

It is unlikely that God would launch us into something long-term that is not within our sphere of gifting and for which we have no training or prior preparation. God will have primed us for what's ahead, even if we only 'catch up' with what He's been doing afterwards. Some of His best work is done behind our backs. If we knew too much we'd interfere.

In the film The Karate Kid Daniel-san is disappointed to be told by his Sensei to sand the wooden decking. This was not the training he hoped for, day after day of this mundane work. It's only later when he defends himself from a blow that he realises the sanding motion has prepared him to block with strength and speed. The Holy Spirit is the best personal trainer we can have!

6. Do practical things line up?

This can be a difficult to discern correctly as sometimes God will ask us to do something that makes no sense at the time, and even trusted friends will not understand. It's only after we take the step of faith that the practical things line up. On other occasions we can see clear practical guidance and issues; money, housing and schooling drawing us into the place and ministry God has for us.

'So then, the word of the LORD to them will become: Do this, do that, a rule for this, a rule for that; a little here, a little there' (Isaiah 28v 13a)

With one foot we walk out our calling, gifting and discipleship and with the other we tread the practicalities of life. Both are God's remit and He will guide us in them both. We are whole beings and our practical needs are important to our Father God (Phil 4v 19) just as our spiritual development is.

7. Does it develop faith?

The Kingdom of God operates by faith. Faith is the currency of the Kingdom and there's no other way to please God. Normally a step forward with God involves a certain amount of risk. When Peter went to the Centurion it was possible that he was walking into a trap (Acts 10), he knew what Roman commanders were capable of. Wherever Paul went there were traps laid for him by those who wanted to drive him out.

'And without faith it is impossible to please God' Hebrews (11v 6a)

If the path we feel led along is always comfortable and blessed, and we are continually thanked, we must question if it is right. It's not good for us always to be within our limits, we need space to grow and adversity to develop us. On the other hand, it's bad theology to think God is always going to ask of us what we don't want to do.

'Take delight in the LORD, and he will give you the desires of your heart'. (Psalm 37v 4)

8. Does it harm anyone?

We can't just drop everything and run because we have heard God. If following God causes us to break our commitments to other people we have to pray this through carefully with integrity and honesty. This might

'It would be better for them to be thrown into the sea with a millstone tied around their neck than to cause one of these little ones to stumble'.
(Luke 17v 2)

require staying in our current job another year or paying off a debt before we go.

If God is in the guidance people may well be willing to be flexible with us, but if they are not, we have to honour our word. Sacrifices have to be made in the kingdom of God, no mistake, but if our decision brings undue suffering for our children or spouse we have to at least question what we think we are hearing. They may need time to hear from God themselves.

9. Is it for now or later on?

'From the tribe of Issachar, there were 200 leaders of the tribe with their relatives. All these men understood the signs of the times and knew the best course for Israel to take'. (1 Chron 12v 32)

In early 2018 I was on a week's mission in Hyderabad, South India, and staying at the flat of my pastor friend. It was a welcome break from my regular pastoring which I was discouraged about. There were disagreements about the way forward and I was feeling increasingly squeezed and generally unhappy.

My friend took me to the local tailor with some white cotton he had bought in the market. We both were measured up and the material was left with the tailor. Two days later two beautiful white shirts were delivered to the flat. I tried mine on; it was quite something, I've never had a made to measure anything. As I was admiring myself in the mirror I heard from God clearly, 'just as this shirt fits you perfectly, it's made to measure, there's a role and a mantle coming for you that will be exactly the same. A perfect fit! The job you've been waiting for all your life.'

This was hard to believe at the time. Was my current job going to change, or was it something new? Something had to give. Between now and then I wondered if **this** (ie. the year in London) was it, but I knew definitively as I got the job of evangelist that this was the role. It was a year and a half between hearing from God until the promise was fulfilled. Not long in God's timing. Some things take much longer! We have said before, timings can be particularly difficult and need to be handled with humility. We think we know, but we could be wrong!

10. Are more people going to hear about Jesus?

'When they came to the border of Mysia, they tried to enter Bithynia, but the Spirit of Jesus would not allow them to'. (Acts 16v 7)

Sometimes when we are desperate to advance into what God has called us to we can inadvertently back ourselves into a corner where we have less influence than before. Paul found that he could not enter Bithynia as the Holy Spirit would not permit it.

Its interesting to speculate what did this 'not allowing' consist of? Was Paul given a dream? Did he have a sense of warning in his spirit, or a message from an angel? Was there a literal block like Balaam encountered as he tried to get through the vineyard?

We do not know definitively, but what we do sense is that God had a better plan. Maybe there was a trap set for Paul in that region, or God knew he would catch a disease there? Possibly the people there were not ready to hear? It wasn't the Kairos (appointed or opportune) time.

'Then the LORD opened Balaam's eyes, and he saw the angel of the LORD standing in the roadway with a drawn sword in his hand. Balaam bowed his head and fell face down on the ground before him'. (Numbers 22v 31)

Jesus left the region of the Gadarenes when asked by the people even though he had just delivered Legion (Luke 8v 37). He did return later, perhaps when the people were ready to hear His message, the demoniac having witnessed of his healing through the region (and all pigs removed to safety!). Sometimes we can get cross with God and feel thwarted, when actually He is protecting us from danger, and ministry that would be wasted. It comes back to trust. In the next chapter we will look at a famous Old Testament prophet who heard unmistakably from God, but didn't want this 'guidance' in his life.

Part 3

Jesus and Prophetic Evangelism

7 Jonah the reluctant prophetic evangelist

Jonah is an Old Testament type of a New Testament prophetic evangelist. Like Paul, who received his call over 700 years later, he was commissioned as a preacher to the Gentiles. The great commission is present in the Old Testament for those with eyes to see. Israel was called to be a light and a priest to the nations (Isa 42v 6). Alas she never fully rose to her great call, but nonetheless we can see glimpses of God's heart for the nations in His dealing with her. Jonah is the first 'overseas' missionary at the time when the world was not made small by planes, trains and automobiles.

'The word of the Lord came to Jonah son of Amittai: "Go to the great city of Nineveh and preach against it, because its wickedness has come up before me." But Jonah ran away from the Lord and headed for Tarshish. He went down to Joppa, where he found a ship bound for that port. After paying the fare, he went aboard and sailed for Tarshish to flee from the Lord'. (Jonah 1v 1–3)

God wanted Jonah to *preach repentance* in Nineveh. This is a good description of the office of evangelist. An evangelist should have the grace to preach a strong and abrupt citywide message, to tell people the worst about themselves in order to precipitate them getting right with God. Jonah's call is prophetic. He was told by God where to go, when and what might happen. God showed him the spiritual state of the Ninevites. Jonah's call was specific, and possibly Jonah received it as a death sentence.

Jonah's mission was groundbreaking when the rest of Israel, if they cared at all, was locked into an 'us and God' mentality, (we are the seed of Abraham (Gal 3v 16)). Granted, Jonah was far from keen about the idea of cross-cultural evangelism. He literally fled in the opposite direction. But one thing he never denied was what the call actually was. We are told very little about the prophecy he was given, unlike most other Old Testament prophetic books. This short book is viewed through his own experience and emotion. We surmise that he was given a message of repentance to preach in Nineveh.

We are given no genealogy for Jonah. However he is held by Rabbinic Jewish tradition to be the widow of Zarephath's son, whom Elijah raised to life again (1 Kings 17). If this is true we could say that after his three days in the belly of the whale he has been raised from death to life twice, a unique feat in Biblical exploits. There is a higher density of miracles to verses in Jonah than any other book in the Bible. They were also prophetic miracles (re. three days and nights in the belly of the fish, foreshadowing Christ's death, burial and resurrection Matt 12v 39-40). But the danger is that the extraordinary miracles divert our attention from the bigger purpose of salvation coming to Nineveh.

The message of repentance from sin is a powerful one that can yield a harvest, anywhere, and at any time. But when it is strategically directed at a specific group of people who need that message and are prepared for it, the results can be extraordinary. Possibly Jonah could have preached his message to some effect in any city, but when directed by God the fruit is multiplied exponentially. The whole city repents with the civic authority leading the way. It's almost unprecedented that a whole city would repent; Nineveh sets an example that Israel could learn from. Jonah was reluctant, rebellious in fact, but none the less eventually he fulfilled his mission and has unprecedented and unrivalled 'success.'

To enlarge on the fish theme in Jonah, seven centuries later, Jesus told His disciples to throw their net out on the other side of the boat, at which point there's such a bumper catch they can hardly pull it in (John 21v 6). Possibly the 'prophetic' instruction to cast the nets on the 'other side' is analogous to Jonah's call to a city like Nineveh where the 'catch' is ready?

The little Jonah inside us

We can all identify with Jonah's raw feelings, and recognise in ourselves the desire to run away from difficulties and confrontations. The church I pastored before my role as evangelist with Through Faith Missions was in a tourist and retirement seaside town. It had a unique demographic, and the average age was high. The town-wide church at the time had few or no children. There was no thriving youth or children's work. I felt this vacuum keenly. God put in me a strong 'prophetic' desire to see the next generation in church and being discipled, which expressed itself largely in prayer and discussion with others.

For years we asked God to raise up, or send in, a youth worker to Hunstanton. I always envisaged that God would either change our financial circumstances so we could employ somebody or raise up someone gifted from within the church. The children weren't coming to church so somebody needed to go to where they were. However, our approaches to the schools were roundly rebuffed if they were even acknowledged.

We all know how dangerous it is in church to suggest an idea, in other people's eyes it's tantamount to volunteering. I had never considered myself a children's worker and still don't. I saw my ministry in other spheres, but we can't 'be precious'. Sometimes it's just about being the person God needs us to be at that moment. God had my heart pointing in the right direction, now all I needed was a 'gentle' shove.

An opportunity opened for 'someone' to join an area team taking Open the Book (a nationally recognised school assembly scheme) into local schools, I couldn't let it go. When this new outlet began, we didn't have Anna our daughter, I am the youngest of three children and I had virtually no experience of children's ministry, just helping out in Sunday school a few times. I learnt rapidly on the job, through many mistakes. A year later, with a change of headmaster, there was suddenly an opening to run a club in the local high school. No one else came forward and it dawned on me reluctantly that the volunteer would have to be me. How did I not see this coming? Teenagers? Really? Teenage ministry is one of those 'specialist' ministries. If you've tried it, you'll know what I mean!

Despite my failings God blessed this ministry, more obviously than my pastoral ministry. At one stage I led an assembly team into nine schools (reception and junior) and was on team for an after-school and lunch club at the high school. I never wanted to go back into that high school, it was my school as a teenager and held bad memories for me.

Once I stepped over this hurdle, which was not without cost, I discovered the high-school team had a difficult dynamic. The paid worker had a completely different idea to me about how overtly 'Christian' it should be. We clashed, and what he said went. It was hard to be sowing myself into something that was certainly not my first choice, when I didn't at least feel free to be myself.

Meanwhile at the reception and junior schools we had to deal with bureaucracy and in some schools our assemblies were the first thing to be dropped if it was inconvenient. Humility was a prerequisite not an optional extra. Several times we turned up with costumes and props only to greeted with, 'Oh no we've got a 'special' assembly today, didn't anyone tell you?' Does a 'sorry' really cost that much?

Also, volunteers were like gold dust and prone to dropping out with no warning. This left me making bricks without straw. Every church thinks children's and youth work is very important, and might give to it financially, but we scraped the barrel to find volunteers. I found it hard not to resent churches and even God. One day I was out for a country walk with Anna in the pushchair. Someone phoned to drop out of the lunch club that day with one hour to go. After hanging up, a shout erupted from deep within me, 'I can't do this anymore God, it's too hard, I can't do it.' God was deafeningly silent. It's always much easier to volunteer for something than to extract yourself, especially if you care about people. I did love the kids (I still pray daily for two of them).That wasn't the issue, it was everything else that went with the club.

The danger is, even if God blesses us with 'success' we can resent people and even God Himself because we feel trapped by the circumstances. We can become disembodied from why we started to do something in the first place!

We're like the little Dutch boy of legend with his finger in that hole in the dyke, preventing his village from being flooded; he is unable to disengage, but is uncomfortable with the whole experience.

'And the Lord's servant must not be quarrelsome but must be kind to everyone, able to teach, not resentful'. (2 Tim 2v 24)

8 Pitfalls of prophetic evangelism

Any type of ministry has pitfalls, specific to its unique challenges. We want to avoid them at all costs in order to stay on the highway of holiness! (Isaiah 40) Like many prophetic evangelists Jonah had a passionate nature. There was nothing remotely half hearted about him! We can discover so much from his reluctant 'journey' into God's purposes – mostly what not to do. We can learn from some specific pitfalls that Jonah did not avoid:

Rejecting the message, running from God

Prophetic evangelism is not something we can turn on and off. There will be times we want to hear what God has to say to us, and welcome it gladly. On other occasions it will be inconvenient and costly to our reputation, we may be misunderstood and even judged by those we most want to think well of us. If we have not understood the cost of ministry we will be indignant, even outraged by this, like Jonah. Most weeks after our school clubs I decided, that's it, this is my last session. It's not my schtick to be cool, the comic, or put up with bad attitudes, *and anyway God it's not my ministry.*

'You deceived me, LORD, and I was deceived; you overpowered me and prevailed. I am ridiculed all day long; everyone mocks me'. (Jeremiah 20v 7)

Once I felt God speak to me clearly about a specific situation which required me to implement a change. This was hugely unpopular, resulted in great misunderstanding and though I gave Him ample opportunity God never retracted what He said. We cannot have it all ways, if we want God to speak to us we must be willing to hear both what suits us endorses our ministry and that which will lead us through the vale of tears. Consider Jeremiah's candid complaint to God, he and Jonah have a lot in common. The difference is Jonah's Gentile audience listened and repented whereas, by and large Jeremiah's Jewish audience who should have known better rejected his message.

Maybe Jonah's ministry would not have been so miserably lonely had he had friends to help give him perspective and remind him how much God had entrusted to him. Ministry can be a heavy and lonely burden, ask Jonah, and even the strongest Christian can succumb to despair without prayer and support. The task is so enormous, we need others to help us with our perspective.

Lonewolf syndrome

'The LORD God said,
"It is not good for the man
to be alone.' (Gen 2v 18a)

Jonah is a singularly desolate figure. His short book starts with him running from God, alone, and concludes with him sitting alone in a bitter lament after God has shown mercy to Nineveh. It is a temptation, and a gravitational pull, for prophetic evangelists to be lone wolves. This is accentuated in the Old Testament where the prophet, or group of prophets operated independently anyway. Prophetic evangelists can be irritants in church. We see the world through our ministry filters which can be unsettling for Christians who want a quiet, calm space. But if we are to bear lasting fruit it is vital we stay in church, instead of stomping off in frustration. Pastors need evangelists and evangelists need pastors; everyone wins if we support and 'sharpen' each other.

Obeying under duress, being an unwilling servant

'Then the word of the Lord came to Jonah a second time: "Go to the great city of Nineveh and proclaim to it the message I give you."Jonah obeyed the word of the Lord and went to Nineveh. Now Nineveh was a very large city; it took three days to go through it. Jonah began by going a day's journey into the city, proclaiming, "Forty more days and Nineveh will be overthrown." The Ninevites believed God. A fast was proclaimed, and all of them, from the greatest to the least, put on sackcloth'. (Jonah 3v 1–5)

Jonah was given a second chance to obey God, and although it wasn't with alacrity, this time he went. It was a long overland journey through dangerous territories towards a cruel historic enemy of Israel. We are told nothing of his travels, which must have taken weeks during which he had plenty of opportunity to turn around. He was surrounded by risks and dangers and initially there would be no welcome for him at Nineveh. We can only imagine how evil the practices were in this city named after a female deity, Ishtar or Jezebel. We know from Elijah's experience how little Jezebel loved the prophets. I wonder if this crosses Jonah's mind on his journey there.

Jonah could have looked at this commission as his big break. *Finally, God is recognising what a gift I am to his Kingdom, at last people are going to know how good I am. I really don't get enough appreciation in Israel, they don't understand what they have in me, now I'll show them.* We can fall into two excesses, if we decide to obey God's call. Either we charge ahead because God has to bless us and we're not going to wait around for Him to get round to giving us specifics. Or we miss perfectly good opportunities because we won't take a step without being specifically 'led'. We say, *I couldn't help that person because I didn't have the greenlight from God. I had to exercise caution and didn't feel the freedom to share.*

I speculate about the parable of the good Samaritan (Luke 10v 25-37). Was the priest bustling off to Jerusalem where God had told him he would find a man in a red cloak drinking water in Solomon's arcade at lunchtime looking for truth? Maybe the Levite was dashing to visit his sick mother between services? Maybe they both felt completely vindicated because God wasn't 'telling' them to help the wounded man, and they were busy about His work. Helping wounded people wasn't their ministry calling?

Selfish use of our gifts

Jonah had a unique paradox to contend with. If his citywide evangelistic campaign was successful, and people seriously repented, his prophetic warning would be proved wrong because God would change His mind. He knew from personal experience that God was merciful and prone to giving second chances. If Jonah's warning came true then it might be too late for anyone to repent. Like Jonah do we care more about our reputation or God getting His will done? It might be that God's call on our life will take us into places where our reputation is trampled underfoot. From Jonah's perspective his call is a lose-lose scenario. He feels justified in his responses. If a similar thing happens to us, our hearts will be exposed. Are we willing to share in the reproach of Christ? (Hebrews 11v 26). Are we fair weather prophetic evangelists, or are we in it for the long haul?

'When God saw what they did and how they turned from their evil ways, he relented and did not bring on them the destruction he had threatened'.
(Jonah 3v 10)

'It is true that some preach Christ out of envy and rivalry, but others out of goodwill. The latter do so out of love, knowing that I am put here for the defence of the gospel. The former preach Christ out of selfish ambition, not sincerely, supposing that they can stir up trouble for me while I am in chains. But what does it matter? The important thing is that in every way, whether from false motives or true, Christ is preached. And because of this I rejoice'.
(Phil 1v 15-18)

If the gospel is preached with less than pure motives it can still work salvation. Jesus said of the Pharisees, 'So you must be careful to do everything they tell you. But do not do what they do, for they do not practise what they preach'. (Matt 23v 3). But how much better to have joyful obedience from a prophetic evangelist who loves the people he's preaching to with God's love, *'I take joy in doing your will, my God, for your instructions are written on my heart.* (Psalm 40v 8)

There can be a use of evangelism and the prophetic that is disembodied from the love of God and the love of people. Tragically some evangelists leave a trail of destruction behind them. We mustn't treat people as a commodity that only exist to validate our ministry. I approached two 'missionaries' behind a literature table in Edinburgh city centre to say hi and encourage them. They did not want my 'encouragement'. Without any pleasantries they sharply demanded if I was a Christian, this was swiftly followed up by an interrogation into how long I read the Bible for that day. The culmination of the conversation was their judgment over me because it wasn't enough. These men were a menace. It's terrifying that they were the public face of Christianity in that city.

Ministering to people we don't love

'But to Jonah this seemed very wrong, and he became angry. He prayed to the Lord, isn't this what I said, Lord, when I was still at home? That is what I tried to forestall by fleeing to Tarshish. I knew that you are a gracious and compassionate God, slow to anger and abounding in love, a God who relents from sending calamity. Now, Lord, take away my life, for it is better for me to die than to live.' (Jonah 4v 1-3)

A pastor friend of mine had a fledgling evangelist in his congregation. She was extremely forceful, impatient, manipulative and gifted as an evangelist. He felt constant pressure to respond to her latest idea which always needed to happen yesterday. He loved evangelism and was more than commonly sympathetic to her but nothing was ever enough. With hindsight he reflected that he spent way too much time trying to keep her happy and engaged, perhaps it was madness to try. But somewhere along the line, he asked himself, did he stop pastorally loving her and start resenting her? He was never responsible for her behaviour, only his own, but he confessed that in the end he saw her as a nuisance. She left in a huff and attacked his reputation wherever she went. Was this inevitable? Maybe, but if we don't love the people we minister to we need to repent before God.

Before I preach I try to pray these three things, fill me with your Spirit Lord, give me your love for these people, and do in them what you have given me to preach about. We must never let ourselves treat people as a commodity or think we're too big for small opportunities. I was on a mission trip to Chiapas, in Southern Mexico and sent to preach at a church plant in Tuxtla Gutierrez while the rest of the mission team went to do an evangelistic service in the mountains. I was looking forward to this opportunity and had prepared well. I expected a reasonable turn out. In Mexico the numbers are usually greater than I was used to in England. It was a long journey and I tried not to let my face fall when we arrived and there were only five people there. Is this all I'm worth? By the time I preached there were nine, it takes a lot more emotional energy to preach to nine than one hundred, it's easier to 'feed' off larger numbers. I prayed the prayer above. In these moments we are reminded that the people are not there to validate our ministry, but we are there to serve them. If we can't be loving to nine, what makes us think we can be loving to one hundred, or a thousand.

Ending up angry with God

I preached in another small church once and was ruffled by how impolite the people were. It's not that I expect anyone to genuflect, but this was off the scale rudeness. As I stood up to speak, there was commotion, people were talking across the room, a couple walked out noisily and others had their heads buried in their smart phones. I felt so disrespected. It's hard to preach when there is no honour. It was hard work, preaching in sinking sand. In the back of my mind I was trying to forgive the congregation and the pastor. How could he allow his congregation to behave like this?

But God said to Jonah, "Is it right for you to be angry about the plant?" "It is," he said. "And I'm so angry I wish I were dead." (Jonah 4v 9)

Afterwards on the way home I spoke to my friend who had come with me, he was senior to me in ministry. I opined about the service, it was dreadful, really difficult spiritually and I didn't connect with the congregation. He commented, 'you let yourself get angry with the congregation didn't you?' I confessed this was true and I remembered trying to keep an angry edge out of my voice. He said 'As soon as you get angry with people you lose them.' My first thought was, "*I never had them in the first place*," but I've never forgotten his point.

The prophetic is a strange thing, we don't understand it fully, and it comes with a price tag. If we don't want to be misunderstood by others it's not the line of work for us. Most of the prophetic figures in the Old and New Testaments are misunderstood, sometimes from a very young age. It rarely improves until much later when everyone can see retrospectively what God has done with their lives, consider Moses or Joseph.

We are not told what Jonah's family and friends thought of his missionary calling to Nineveh. Almost certainly they would have been sceptical, if not hostile to it. 'You're completely wrong Jonah, God wouldn't send you to that pagan lot, there're our enemies. They'll kill you, or worse'. Much like Noah, Jonah almost certainly had to swallow mockery and disappointment. 'We thought you were going to do great things Jonah, but you're wasting your talent on this! God didn't resurrect you (twice!) just so you could waste yourself on them.'

We have to remember that when we gave our lives to Jesus we gave Him the right to decide how they are spent. How much we receive of blessing and affirmation as opposed to hardship and suffering is God's sole concern. We must trust that He is doing far more with our lives than we currently realise, and must be more jealous for His reputation than our own.

Self pity party

"Pity me, pity me, O you my friends, For the hand of God has struck me'. (Job 19v 21)

There are few things less edifying than a Christian in his or her mission field having a pity party! Jonah does it in style! At the end of his book we don't find him celebrating with the Ninevites and leading them in exuberant worship but licking his wounds outside the city. '*Nobody appreciates me, no one cares how hard it is for me, no one knows how much I am giving. If I had any friends I'd invite them to wallow in misery with me'.* If we once open ourselves a crack to self-pity it will slide in like a venomous snake to poison our hearts and asphyxiate us.

Once we were hosting a mission team at The Way Church and several members came along to the lunch club at the high school, which had been running for a year. It was the first club of the school year and was well attended. The school had publicized it and we had our highest attendance, over twenty. I thought it went well, the kids were boisterous as always, but we tended to gather the needy kids. We recognised that sometimes they used us as a hideaway, but that was fine if they came. I thought the team would be impressed.

After the club the mission team debriefed, I was in for a shock. Their leader thought it was terrible, the behaviour was unacceptable and the club itself needed 'loads of work'. I was tempted to pull a 'Jonah'. It hurt to hear their comments. I'd fought tooth and nail to keep that club afloat. I was working with someone who didn't share my evangelical fervour and I felt continually blocked. I couldn't lead it as I wanted, and the dynamic was very complicated. We'd held on by a thread through shaky months with only two or three attending. We had no budget, everything we did was self-funded. I'd never chosen this ministry in the first place. The 'defence lawyer' in my mind sprang into full denial mode, pointing and accusing!

These mission team members were comparing our humble effort with their large well-resourced youth club, full of well-behaved middle class Christian kids. This was my theory. But I had a choice, the 'Jonah' route; down to the bottom of the garden to eat worms? Or, do I say, I can always learn, they're right this club could be better? They didn't know all the history, how could they? They spoke as they found. I resisted the temptation to tell them the troubled history of the club, thereby justifying myself, but their opinions stung like crazy.

As I separated out my personal feelings from the facts, I knew they weren't being vindictive, just honest because they wanted the club to succeed. I should have humbled myself and asked for their advice, I confess I didn't get that far. These are defining moments, when we silently grow, or angrily turn our backs on God and our Christian friends. Let's overcome!

What do we learn from all this?

We must learn to take our praise and affirmation direct from God. If we're waiting for someone else to thank us, we may end up like Jonah on the mountain overlooking Nineveh, shaking our fist at everyone, including God. People only see a tiny part of the picture but God sees the whole and therefore only He can accurately judge. It's nice when what we do is noticed and even applauded by others, but this can't be our motivation.

I wonder why Jonah didn't head straight back to Israel if he was so unhappy? Could it be that he knew there would only be more misunderstanding and judgement there? No-one would recognise how faithful he had been, they wouldn't be any happier about Nineveh's repentance than he was. Well, God noticed Jonah, and he gets a personal mention from Jesus in the New Testament! Jesus prophesied His imminent death using Jonah's experience.

If we're going to be successful long term in prophetic evangelism we have to be able to function without constant affirmation from people. We stand in a long line of saints who weren't understood in their own lifetime. We can only stay balanced if we are not inflated with pride when we are complemented or crushed when we are criticised. We must embrace the pain of being misunderstood, just as Jesus did

'For as Jonah was three days and three nights in the belly of a huge fish, so the Son of Man will be three days and three nights in the heart of the earth'. (Matthew 12v 40)

on the cross. Our reputation is most important in heaven, where there is twenty twenty vision, rather than on earth where snap judgements are made. Even our most trusted friends can't fully evaluate our ministry. What Jesus says about us is supreme. If we learn that God's 'well done, good and faithful servant' is enough, we are insulated from the capricious opinions of man. We can continue without their endorsement and regardless of their criticism.

Success in Nineveh?

'But the Lord said, "You have been concerned about this plant, though you did not tend it or make it grow. It sprang up overnight and died overnight. And should I not have concern for the great city of Nineveh, in which there are more than a hundred and twenty thousand people who cannot tell their right hand from their left—and also many animals?" (Jonah 4v 10–11)

I'm praying that one day someone will tap me on the back and say, you don't remember me, but you brought Christian assemblies into my school twenty years ago. I'm a pastor/missionary/Christian doctor now. I wouldn't be here now if you hadn't taught us about God, there was no-one else in my life to tell me, you and your team were the only ones.

At one point our combined clubs and Open the Book assemblies were delivering the gospel to six to seven hundred children a month. We built a good enough rapport with the younger kids that they would cheer with excitement when we arrived, groan if they were told we weren't coming next month and shout hello across the High Street! There were also Christian children we could encourage, especially the younger ones who weren't embarrassed to be identified.

Notwithstanding the other team difficulties, God gave me an excellent co-worker with whom I am still good friends. God gave us a great love for the children, we spent hours interceding for them and the work continues after I moved on to a new position in a new area. There is a legacy! It is one of the highest privileges to hold out the word of life to children who might otherwise never hear it. To introduce broken and hurting children and teenagers to Jesus is just about as good as it gets!

'Truly I tell you, anyone who will not receive the kingdom of God like a little child will never enter it." (Mark 10v 15)

9 Journey into prophetic evangelism

It's a mystery how God gives us different gifts and develops us in them according to His will and in His perfect timing. His timings are perfect even if they are curious to us. (1 Cor 12v 11). I was brought up in churches that wouldn't mention the prophetic, and might even see it as something strange or wrong. There wasn't a lot of encouragement to expect God could, or would, speak to you directly. Direct

'For now we see only a reflection as in a mirror; then we shall see face to face. Now I know in part; then I shall know fully, even as I am fully known'. (1 Cor 13v 12)

evangelism didn't always happen either, although there was plenty of what I would now call friendship evangelism.

I experienced a lot of new things as I spent time in a charismatic Baptist Church. When Bec and I got married in 2003 I started attending her charismatic fellowship, which became my spiritual home. At first, I was resistant and my poor wife had to put up with my opinionated views and suspicions. God moved me along in stages, He and others were patient and gracious with me.

There was a very strong missional ethos in my new church, which I did approve of although it wasn't comfortable. Through the years there wasn't much that we didn't try evangelistically, with mixed results. We conducted outdoor services and baptisms in the sea, carol singing, 'Treasure Hunting', leafleting, invitation barbecues and men's breakfasts. One year three or four of us knocked on every door in the town (4000 homes) with a Mark's gospel and offered prayer. Evangelism was an integral part of who we were, it wouldn't have occurred to us not to do it. I am pretty slow on the uptake and didn't realise that God was calling me to full time evangelism. I was late to my own party!

One of my favourite things was 'coffee evangelism'. In our coffee lounge on a sunny day it would be lovely to sit outside and share a drink with someone. Knowing that there was time for conversation really suited me, and a guest would 'settle in' and then naturally would inquire who we were, and why were we doing what we were doing? This set things up well to share faith.

The visiting prophet

There was another first for me, a 'prophet' coming to visit. The church was buzzing, an American speaker was coming to do a Friday evening meeting. He had a reputation for accurately telling people about their lives and what God was going to do. I was secretly terrified. Was he going to call out some dreadful sin even I didn't know about in my life?

There was also the possibility we'd hear something juicy about someone else. If I didn't go, people might jump to the wrong conclusions, or so I thought. I cringed when he scrutinised me long and hard, but he was encouraging in what he said. How little I understood the prophetic gift and what motivates it. The evening came and went, and it wasn't scary, quite exciting actually.

As God was drawing me into the prophetic, He developed more of an edge to my evangelism. At the coffee shop God would lead me to share a part of my testimony, or a relevant Bible portion which would sometimes lead to a disclosure from the person or people I told. They'd say, 'I haven't told this to anyone but I feel I can share it now,' or 'can you pray for my daughter who suffers with terrible anxiety'. Sometimes God would give a word of knowledge which would result in praying for healing.

Fast forward ten years and not only was I going to 'prophetic' meetings, but I was the one teaching and prophesying to them. God led me along mysterious paths to meet some extraordinary people on the way to where he was taking me. Potentially, I am now the person that others would be terrified of because I might spot some terrible fault in them! Well I never do see much of that, because fortunately for us God is so generous, and always searches for the best in us. He's been far more generous to me in prophetic words than I've deserved. Even if I did see 'sin' in someone it's very unlikely it would be mentioned; more likely I'd pray about it privately later.

Intuition or the prophetic?

It's a challenge to discern between intuition and the prophetic. Bec and I are atypical in our marriage; I'm the intuitive one. She's logical, ordered, and scientific in analysing things, and I am incredibly grateful for her gift. She can help me unload all the emotion I've picked up from people and bring me back to the facts. We can go to the same family gathering or meet with friends, and on the way back I'll say, 'what is wrong with cousin Jade?' She'll reply, 'what do you mean, she's fine?' 'No, there's something wrong' I insist.

Sometimes I am right, sometimes wrong, and other times we never find out. Weeks later we hear something about a friend and I look at Bec, 'do you remember what I said when we saw them last?' She'd concede 'you were right, how did you know?'

There is a thin line between intuition and the prophetic but working together they are compelling. After a powerful experience of being filled with the Holy Spirit my 'intuition,' if that's what it was, became more acute. When I was commissioned as senior pastor at The Way, pastor Bill Isaacs, a good friend and experienced minister came and spoke to me afterwards. 'God is giving you three gifts; the word of knowledge, the word of wisdom and especially the discerning of spirits'. These all fall into the general category of the prophetic; knowing and speaking gifts.

I am not infallible, far from it, but often on meeting someone I get a strong feeling about them. Mostly this is positive; I really like their spirit, and then as I get to know them naturally I realise why. Occasionally I get a red-light warning in my spirit about someone, even though they seem so nice, and this has been proved right a few times.

A season of revelation

It is not always clear why God deals with us in certain ways at certain times. 'His paths are beyond tracing out' (Romans 11v 33b). We sometimes only know that He is to be trusted, and if He is working in a particular way there is a good reason. I've learnt to drink in all the water of the Holy Spirit that I can in a season of blessing, because rather like a camel, if I have a desert to cross later on I want to be prepared.

'How I long for the months gone by, for the days when God watched over me, when his lamp shone on my head and by his light I walked through darkness!' (Job 29v 2-3)

For one four to five month season God seemed to be speaking to me all the time, especially as I was going to sleep at night, precious revelation which I'm still living off. God often speaks to me in pictures; in scripture God often spoke to his Prophets in a kind of prophetic picture language (they were called Nabi prophets– Seers). In this season, night after night, God was pouring revelation like honey into my heart. The next morning I would rush for my journal and write down, to the best of my ability, what He had told me. I look back at these entries years later and realise how many things have come to pass.

Sometimes I crave being able to go back into a season like that. It was so precious, and God felt so near even though I didn't understand everything that was happening. I'm not sure I was being rewarded for anything, or that I had done anything wrong when the daily revelations stopped, it seemed to be a season that had run its course. It's inevitable that we would want to stay in seasons of blessing with God, and rush through the painful and testing ones. Discipleship is an adventure over mountains and through valleys! I also regret not recording more accurately what God was saying, sometimes I didn't remember everything in the morning.

I can't recall the first time someone commented to me 'you're a prophetic person', but somewhere along the line people started saying it regularly. I could be in a prayer meeting and think, we must pray for John Brown; and at that moment somebody starts to do just that. Particularly when I was around people with the same areas of gifting as me prophetic things would happen. I would think, it'd be great to speak to so-and-so, and then lo and behold she would phone up out the blue. Or I might feel a pain in my body to show me what someone else was feeling and needed healing for. Personal prophecy was something that I started to flow in, and I could prophesy over a group with some degree of accuracy. To do this over 'strangers' was life-affirming, because as a pastor there's so much 'information' you store up about your 'flock'. It's hard to separate information from revelation.

Examples of prophetic behaviour

The prophetic is hard to sum up so let's try some examples. Below we encounter four hypothetical characters who are prophetic in the general sense of being spiritually tuned in, seeing or hearing God in a particular way. For instance, we could argue that a word of knowledge is not prophecy because it deals with past or current 'knowledge.' However, it is prophetic in the general sense of 'hearing' or 'seeing' something from God. Discerning of spirits is not direct prophecy, but it is 'spiritual' knowledge that can only come from God through His Holy Spirit.

We can move in a low level of the prophetic without even realising it. We might call it a hunch or a gut-feeling that causes us to change what we were about to do. The leading of God can be so natural that we hardly notice we are being led.

1. The Godly prayer warrior

Everyone's been in a prayer meeting when a Godly and respected old lady says, 'I really feel we need to pray for brother Steve in Kenya right now.' This is irrespective of denomination, ecclesiology, or personal preference. She might be in a church that doesn't even believe in the prophetic, or wouldn't encourage it. It later transpires that brother Steve was in a standoff with militants who want a bribe from the church orphanage. Suddenly, things improved round about the time the prayer started; he says thanks and please keep praying.

2. The prophetic youth worker

She might say to her teenage group, today instead of doing our usual car cleaning I believe God wants us to buy three trays of doughnuts and take them into town to distribute. Let's all pray and write down a verse on a card which we can hand out with the doughnuts. The youth end the evening buzzing with what God is doing and pleading, 'Can we do it again next week?' People are released into areas of their gifting, and want to invite their friends next time. A youth worker who wasn't prophetic could do this, but it's less likely, and there wouldn't be the sense of freshness and excitement to it.

3. The prophetic artist

He paints a ship in a storm and most people who view it have a sense of being brought into God's presence. They have a scripture verse come to mind and ask what the storm represents, because it relates to their story. Our friend Chris Duffet from Great Gransden is amongst many other things a prophetic artist. He kindly gave us a print of one of his paintings of a lighthouse. It sits proudly in our front room, and whenever I look at it I get something fresh from God. An artist of comparable skill level can paint the same subject with beautiful results but those who view it don't talk about God or have a Bible verse, they reflect on the technique of the painting.

4. The prophetic evangelist

Last but certainly not least, she may use the same materials as other evangelists but there is an unusual sense of God's presence and the conversation is more likely to take an unexpected turn. She doesn't work in a straight line but draws connections and patterns from things that other people wouldn't necessarily notice. She might be among the first to pick up on the overall spiritual atmosphere in a town, and what has gone on historically. She can connect this information, and brings the 'big' picture to how individual people are reacting to the open air service or door knocking.

APPENDIX 3 provides further, more detailed, examples of the range of prophetic tools that God graciously provides.

APPENDIX 9 encourages us to the idea that ministry in the prophetic is very truly a journey, from the time we enter into God's Kingdom and as we then mature and grow deeper into Him.

10 *Learning to fly*

Like all good teachers Jesus lets us try out our learning in a safe and nurturing environment. We have some pastor friends from East Anglia called Margaret and Tony Cornell. They'd often visit our old church in the summer combined with a day out at the seaside and were, without fail, an inspiration and encouragement to me. My heart always leapt when they came in because they are people of faith and as pastors could really understand the dynamics of a church like ours. We had a spiritual connection even if we only saw them once a year.

"If you have raced with men on foot and they have worn you out, how can you compete with horses? If you stumble in safe country, how will you manage in the thickets by the Jordan?" (Jer 12v 5)

I can't remember how I first heard, the Christian community is very small world, but I was shocked and saddened to hear in 2017 that Margaret had stage IV lymphoma. She was in her early seventies and was otherwise strong but had been given only two months to live. I didn't think any sickness or disease would dare get anywhere near to them, they both regularly prayed for the sick and had seen significant breakthroughs in their ministry. They were strong in spirit.

At this time I was travelling to London once a month to join an intercession group called 'Prayer for Parliament' that convened in the Houses of Parliament. My route out of East Anglia took me within three miles of their village. The inner 'nudge' to drop in and pray for Margaret kept occurring to me. It had been with me for weeks.

I felt a good deal of resistance, my confidence was not at a high ebb in pastoring. My mind was assailed with lies; 'Who do you think you are?' 'Do you think you have anything special to pray?' I felt condemned at my record of praying for the sick.

As a card carrying Charismatic, I always offered prayer but I confess that I found myself robotically praying for the same people repeatedly with diminishing faith. 'Margaret and Tony have plenty of faith, they don't need help from the likes of you.' They had pastored a much larger church, and were recognised across the county in Christian circles. Did I really think I had anything to offer them? They were 'breakthrough people'. Those lies again; 'when you pray for people, they get worse, best leave them alone.'

But I am an activist, so I phoned them and was pleasantly surprised; they were genuinely grateful to accept my offer. So I found their bungalow, dropped-in, and we talked for a while; Margaret was feeling considerably better. She had recently had the fourth of six chemotherapy courses planned, and the lymphoma was retreating. Still, I was shocked at how much weight she had lost and she was wearing a wig. She was her resolute self though, full of faith. Tony and Margaret built up my faith, not the other way around. 'As iron sharpens iron, so one person sharpens another.' (Prov 27v 17)

We had a powerful time, it was so easy to agree in faith with them both. I anointed Margaret with oil and prayed with all the faith in my heart. As I anointed her, Margaret simultaneously felt a wind of the Holy Spirit blow right through her removing the last traces of cancer. She did not tell me all this at the time but before I left we worshipped together. Off I went to London, blessed to have seen them, but not expecting much. Perhaps if nothing else it was a good for them to know that someone from further afield cared?

Life carried on and I thought very little more about this episode, just sending one or two texts, I was busy and didn't want to pester them. Several months later a glamorous couple walked into our church on a summer morning. I did a double take, surely not, it couldn't be? Margaret and Tony! Margaret looked a good ten years younger, dressed like a film star in a leather jacket, she'd put some weight back on and was beaming light all over her face. Quickly she asked if she could share testimony in the service, 'Gladly' I said.

At this time I was wrestling with feelings of failure as a pastor, as I looked around I wasn't seeing the breakthrough I wanted, quite the reverse. The church was shrinking, and as any pastor will testify, this can be painful even if you know God is moving people on. After worship Margaret stood up, it was hard to imagine that she had been desperately ill so recently.

She gave testimony about her diagnosis and treatment and finally about my visit. I was a little surprised about this. As I had prayed for her all those months ago, apparently she had felt the last bit of cancer leave her body. She knew it was gone, and this was confirmed by her doctor when she was next tested. He couldn't find anything. Wow! What an incredible miracle and a huge boost for me, a ringing endorsement in front of the congregation. The lovely thing was Margaret had medical evidence verifying this miracle, there was nothing 'flaky' about it. Her recovery from the effects of the chemotherapy was also unprecedented in its rapidity, definitely of God!

God let me try out some prophetic 'evangelism' on some very supportive Christians, although they didn't actually have to be led in a prayer of salvation. We've all got to start somewhere. I'd never take that kind of leap of faith in the marketplace with non-Christians if I hadn't first tried it out in a safer context. We have to realistic about working our way up to 'Acts'-like prophetic evangelism in accomplishable stages.

What happens when the prophetic combines with the evangelistic gift?

> 'For the word of God is alive and active. Sharper than any double-edged sword, it penetrates even to dividing soul and spirit, joints and marrow; it judges the thoughts and attitudes of the heart'.
> (Hebrews 4v 12)

In picture form I saw two burning hot coals from the altar in heaven (Isa 6v 6). One represented the gift of evangelism and the other one the gift of prophecy. I held them in either hand where both were flaming and full of power. But when I brought the two together and they touched there was an explosive flame which went ten times higher than the individual flames. The two gifts combined are dynamite, and can break through uniquely, they are explosive in power. For the sake of the lost let's ask God for more of this wonderful gift……

"Whoever can be trusted with very little can also be trusted with much'
(Luke 16v 10)

(see schematic on following page).

Prophetic/Evangelism
complimentary sides of the same coin

PROPHETIC	EVANGELISM
Deliberately 'leaning' into God for revelation concerning the person/people we seek to evangelise. The prophetic 'personalises' the timeless message of the gospel. Truth explodes into the present!	Skilful sharing of the gospel in creative ways on all occasions. The same core message – different expressions. Evangelism pivots from and informs the prophetic gift as the Spirit leads.

Fig 4

This schematic reminds us that the prophetic in general and the task of evangelism in particular can (should?) represent 'two sides of the same coin'. The prophetic is a gifting. Evangelism is a task for all believers. This combination is a powerful way to reach those who are seeking Jesus, those who do not know they are seeking Jesus, and even those who are re-sisting Jesus.

11 Jesus the prophetic evangelist

'Now there was a Pharisee, a man named Nicodemus who was a member of the Jewish ruling council. He came to Jesus at night and said, "Rabbi, we know that you are a teacher who has come from God. For no one could perform the signs you are doing if God were not with him."

Jesus replied, "Very truly I tell you, no one can see the kingdom of God unless they are born again."

"How can someone be born when they are old?" Nicodemus asked. "Surely they cannot enter a second time into their mother's womb to be born!"

Jesus answered, "Very truly I tell you, no one can enter the kingdom of God unless they are born of water and the Spirit. Flesh gives birth to flesh, but the Spirit gives birth to spirit. You should not be surprised at my saying, 'You must be born again.' The wind blows wherever it pleases. You hear its sound, but you cannot tell where it comes from or where it is going. So it is with everyone born of the Spirit."

"How can this be?" Nicodemus asked.

"You are Israel's teacher," said Jesus, "and do you not understand these things? Very truly I tell you, we speak of what we know, and we testify to what we have seen, but still you people do not accept our testimony. I have spoken to you of earthly things and you do not believe; how then will you believe if I speak of heavenly things? No one has ever gone into heaven except the one who came from heaven—the Son of Man. Just as Moses lifted up the snake in the wilderness, so the Son of Man must be lifted up, that everyone who believes may have eternal life in him."

For God so loved the world that he gave his one and only Son, that whoever believes in him shall not perish but have eternal life. For God did not send his Son into the world to condemn the world, but to save the world through him. Whoever believes in him is not condemned, but whoever does *not believe stands condemned already because they have not believed in the name of God's one and only Son. This is the verdict: Light has come into the world, but people loved darkness instead of light because their deeds were evil. Everyone who does evil hates the light, and will not come into the light for fear that their deeds will be exposed. But whoever lives by the truth comes into the light, so that it may be seen plainly that what they have done has been done in the sight of God'.* (John 3v1–21)

At first glance we could surmise that this conversation which Jesus has with Nicodemus is not prophetic evangelism, more prophetic teaching. However, with closer inspection we realise that Nicodemus represents that group of people we might call the 'frozen chosen'. They've grown up in church. Maybe their dad was a vicar or their mum was the worship leader, and everybody knows them. They studied divinity at University and have a robust understanding of different theological positions, fundamentalist, liberal or evangelical. They could discuss the trinity, the resurrection, the rapture and the millennium without missing a beat. They've not ever done anything really bad and they are well liked at church where they regularly attend but they are still NOT a Christian. Sometimes they exude an air of entitlement and no-one would really want to challenge them, they're good givers too!

It's so easy to jump to conclusions, but we are far more effective prophetic evangelists if we assume nothing. As the late Keith Green pithily puts it 'going to church doesn't make you a Christian anymore than going to McDonalds makes you a hamburger'. The late Billy Graham was very successful evangelising people around the fringes of the Anglican Church. Maybe they came from generations of church goers and were faithful in their way, but they'd never made a personal decision for Christ. They were so much part of the furniture that no-one got around to telling them.

There's no need to judge them, or bemoan this fact, only to hold out before them the word of life and invite them to respond. We can't know the state of anybody else's heart unless God shows us. Let's never assume a group of 'Christians' don't need the gospel or that they won't respond if they are given a chance. Nicodemus is in this category (for all his credentials) and Jesus more directly leads him to a 'conversion' point than almost anyone else He speaks to in the gospels. We are left to speculate whether Nicodemus did convert at this point. When someone with that sort of background becomes a true believer, truly it is an awesome thing.

Our preconception can be that prophetic evangelism is all about going and doing; actively seeking out people. Sometimes it is just as important to be still enough in God's presence to let people come to us. My best conversations are when people have come to me, when I'm not looking for it, and sometimes when it isn't convenient. God gave me a picture once which showed me looking perfectly still and at ease in the middle of a large empty room. He showed me that when I was living in his 'stillness' (Psalm 46v 10) people would start to gather around me and I could teach them. They would gravitate to me not the other way round, it would be counterproductive for me to approach them.

He said to them, "Therefore every teacher of the law who has become a disciple in the kingdom of heaven is like the owner of a house who brings out of his storeroom new treasures as well as old." (Matt 13v 52)

Jesus let Nicodemus come to him; He didn't blow his cover or belittle him. Jesus is not so flattered to be visited that He burbles on mindlessly, as we might; He is perfectly composed. This is pure speculation, but maybe God had shown Jesus that Nicodemus was coming, or Jesus had heard a rumour to that effect. He seems unsurprised. Allowing Nicodemus to 'make the move' gave him a sense of initiative or control over the situation; he came at night no doubt to avoid too many people seeing. Perhaps he wanted to find Jesus alone. He appears as a genuine seeker, who has not come to entrap Jesus like his colleagues, and maybe he wouldn't be noticed fraternising with these rough Galileans. What follows is an excellent example of prophetic evangelism.

Nicodemus was part of the spiritual elite in Israel, used to breathless plaudits for his inspired interpretations of the law. He was greeted loudly in the marketplace and ushered to the best seat (Matt 23v 6). He was the Jewish equivalent of Billy Graham, John Stott or C.S. Lewis, 'You are Israel's teacher,' the sharpest and most educated mind. Jesus wasn't in awe of Nicodemus or fooled by his 'spirituality. He saw straight through to the heart. Jesus is dismayed that he, of all people, who ought to understand spiritual realities must be taken back to the spiritual nursery school. Nicodemus comes not to trap or trick Jesus but with genuine hunger, and for his humility he will be amply rewarded.

Jesus is patient, not chiding, ignoring a compliment, or was it flattery? Perhaps this was a windy evening and they were sitting outside, or they could hear the wind howling from inside. This is the only mention in the gospels of being 'born again', a phrase that has proved controversial in recent times. How humbling for Israel's great teacher to be told he must become a babe again. Jesus uses the wind as a metaphor for the invisible activity of the Holy Spirit. We see the result of it, we see a tree bending and leaves rustling, but not the wind itself. Jesus is teaching prophetically. The

Holy Spirit has not yet been poured out in a general sense, that's a future event at Pentecost. In the Old Testament the Spirit anoints for a task and a role but He is not living within all believers. It is Jesus, triumphant in resurrection and ascended to the Father's right hand, Who asks for the Spirit to be poured out. Jesus teaches Nicodemus about Pentecost and beyond, seemingly before His disciples.

Jesus goes on to use a famous episode from Israel's history to prophesy what He will achieve on the Cross of Calvary. Moses held up a bronze serpent (bronze, a metal associated with judgement in Numbers 21), a picture of Christ on the cross swallowing up the work of satan, becoming a curse, and absorbing all the poison of our sin. The Israelites were cured from fiery snake bites as they looked at the serpent. We are saved as we look with faith at the work of the cross. ***"The work of God is this: to believe in the one he has sent."*** (John 6v 29) How often did Nicodemus think back to this conversation after the Cross, realising the full extent of what Jesus was teaching him? Was Nicodemus there in the shadows at Pentecost where the wind of the Spirit blew so fiercely?

'It is the glory of God to conceal a matter; to search out a matter is the glory of kings'. (Prov 25v 2) Nicodemus is entrusted with beautiful wisdom. Jesus pours out His treasures; the Holy Spirit, the Cross, new birth and light for darkness. It is a delightful irony that a learned religious scholar of Israel must be instructed in the basics of how to follow God. Jesus finishes with a gentle rebuke, concerning Nicodemus choosing to visit at night, 'people loved darkness instead of light.' Or is it an invitation to 'go public' with his burgeoning faith? We make much of Jesus' harshness with the Pharisees, and His invective against them (Matt 23). But here He shows the upmost courtesy and respect. Jesus did not trumpet this amazing teaching from a mountainside to multitudes, but to one Pharisee. Possibly a few disciples, including John, overheard.

Nicodemus was given the blueprint for Salvation before the church itself; and told of the death of Christ before the disciples. In this exchange we receive John 3v 16, the verse most synonymous with evangelical Christianity. It's clear that God's work continued in Nicodemus' life after this encounter. He along with Joseph of Arimathea claimed the body of Jesus from Pilate and embalmed it for burial (John 19). He risked the ire of the other religious leaders to honour the dead body of 'Israel's teacher'.

John's gospel records many conversations. In our next chapter we enjoy another one with a Samaritan woman. Both of these examples of prophetic evangelism have similarities, although Jesus is dealing with people at either end of the social and religious spectrum. He skilfully utilises natural objects and nature to reveal profound spiritual truths.

12 *Undone by Jesus*

Now he had to go through Samaria. So he came to a town in Samaria called Sychar, near the plot of ground Jacob had given to his son Joseph. Jacob's well was there, and Jesus, tired as he was from the journey, sat down by the well. It was about noon.

When a Samaritan woman came to draw water, Jesus said to her, "Will you give me a drink?" (His disciples had gone into the town to buy food.)

The Samaritan woman said to him, "You are a Jew and I am a Samaritan woman. How can you ask me for a drink?" (For Jews do not associate with Samaritans).

Jesus answered her, "If you knew the gift of God and who it is that asks you for a drink, you would have asked him and he would have given you living water."

"Sir," the woman said, "you have nothing to draw with and the well is deep. Where can you get this living water? Are you greater than our father Jacob, who gave us the well and drank from it himself, as did also his sons and his livestock?"

Jesus answered, "Everyone who drinks this water will be thirsty again, but whoever drinks the water I give them will never thirst. Indeed, the water I give them will become in them a spring of water welling up to eternal life."

The woman said to him, "Sir, give me this water so that I won't get thirsty and have to keep coming here to draw water."

He told her, "Go, call your husband and come back."

"I have no husband," she replied.

Jesus said to her, "You are right when you say you have no husband. The fact is, you have had five husbands, and the man you now have is not your husband. What you have just said is quite true. "Sir," the woman said, "I can see that you are a prophet. Our ancestors worshipped on this mountain, but you Jews claim that the place where we must worship is in Jerusalem."

"Woman," Jesus replied, "believe me, a time is coming when you will worship the Father neither on this mountain nor in Jerusalem. You Samaritans worship what you do not know; we worship what we do know, for salvation is from the Jews. Yet a time is coming and has now come when the true worshippers will worship the Father in Spirit and in truth, for they are the kind of worshippers the Father seeks. God is spirit, and his worshippers must worship in Spirit and in truth." The woman said, "I know that Messiah" (called Christ) "is coming. When he comes, he will explain everything to us. Then Jesus declared, "I, the one speaking to you – I am he." (John 4v 1-14)

Jesus and His disciples not only were passing through Samaria, but they weren't rushing (like the priest and Levite in the parable of the good Samaritan). So much about this prophetic encounter is counter-cultural and revolutionary. Firstly Jesus and His disciples are travelling through Samaria: a region populated by the progeny of intermarriages and extramarital relations between Jews and Assyrians (720 BC). They are a mongrel race, shunned as morally inferior and unclean. Samaritans were a stench in Jewish nostrils; a reminder of a painful and shameful episode in their history. They gave as good as they got, hating the Jews back. The Pharisaic practice of brushing the dust from their feet originates from removing the contamination from this region if they had to pass through.

The journey wasn't a 'necessary evil'. Jesus and the disciples stopped at Jacob's well, a place purchased by Jacob from Shechem (Gen 33v 19). It's steeped in patriarchal history (Joseph is buried nearby Josh 24v 32, Mount Ebal is close Deut 11v 29). There's something about being evangelistic and prophetic that gets you to the right place at the right time. Jesus is a masterful friendship evangelist, and a prophet.

Remember a Jewish man would not normally interact socially with a strange woman, especially in public. Jesus' ministry continually challenges the social norms regarding women and embraces every opportunity to affirm and uplift them. Small wonder that women ran to Him, and loved Him so much. They still do.

But this encounter is surely beyond the pale? The Samaritan woman is at the well alone at noon, the hottest part of the day. Normally village women would go together to the well just after sunrise and then again at sunset. There would be safety in numbers from bandits and unwanted male attention, and fellowship in their travelling together. Why is this woman out alone at midday?

His interaction with the woman is so natural. Immediately He puts her at ease by asking a favour of her, for her to draw water (echoes of Eliezer and Rebecca Gen 24?). By putting Himself in her debt, He indicates a desire to converse as equals. This is no threatening command. It's human to want to relate to people from a position of strength, where we are the givers! It takes humility to be the recipient of kindness and hospitality.

We discover through Jesus' word of knowledge that she had five husbands and the man she is now with is not her husband. Almost certainly she is an outcast from the female contingent of the community, viewed with a mixture of hatred, hostility and fear. Maybe she has reason to fear for her physical safety if she tries to mingle with them? Ex-wives and their friends would hardly welcome this man-stealer. To say she had a 'complicated past' would be an understatement. What's more, as a woman of questionable morals she might even be out to attract attention from shepherds and farmers and solicit them at their leisure (Song of Songs 1v 7, Ruth 3).

On every level Jesus is prophetic in reaching out to her; crossing a huge social divide that separates them, He brings her into a Kingdom that welcomes and values women from every ethnicity and walk of life. Women will play a key part in the Kingdom of God and this Samaritan will be among the first. No longer to be downtrodden and sidelined by those who 'love the law', but with no law of love.

John is the only gospel writer to include this encounter; she is given a teaching masterclass, equal to the one Jesus had given to Nicodemus. Jesus is no discriminator for, or against, persons. He concludes this encounter with the earliest and the most direct affirmation of His true identity that He gives to anyone. He does not consider her 'a swine' from whom to withhold His pearls; but a worthy recipient of His highest truths. Suffice to say that His disciples are shocked when they return to find Jesus conversing with her.

Jesus is prophetic. He gives a couple of words of knowledge (not explicitly prophecy, which tends to relate to current or future events) which quickly pierces her religious façade. It's interesting that a woman of her moral provenance seeks a defence in religiosity. Why did Jesus use this evangelistic approach with her? Possibly because prophecy gets 'to the heart' very quickly. An intellectual or philosophical approach might have triggered her inner defence mechanism. She wanted to pivot in that direction, back to her comfort zone. Jesus, as always, is the perfect balance of grace and truth. We sense their friendship and trust growing like a watered plant.

The answer to her question, 'Are you greater than our father Jacob?' is, of course, a resounding YES! Jacob may have dug a well to quench the physical thirst of the local people, but Jesus brings spiritual water for people to drink in a barren wilderness of doubt, fear and empty religiosity. Living water that will satisfy eternally.

"Let anyone who is thirsty come to me and drink. Whoever believes in me, as Scripture has said, rivers of living water will flow from within them.'
(John 7v 37–38)

Jesus segues into a teaching for His disciples while this missionary Samaritan woman brings the whole village, *"Come, see a man who told me everything I ever did. Could this be the Messiah?"* (John 4v 29). The village must have been impressed with an immediate transformation in this woman as she was not in a position to command. Her face was glowing and she could look them in the eyes for the first time in years, the shame gone. I would love to know all that Jesus did in the two days He stayed, faith must have been riding very high. And what became of the woman, and which man, if any did she end up with? We can only speculate; with prophetic evangelism we do our part and may never know the end of the story.

They said to the woman, "We no longer believe just because of what you said; now we have heard for ourselves, and we know that this man really is the Saviour of the world." (John 4 v 42)

What can Jesus teach us about prophetic evangelism?

Live in the moment, flow with the Spirit

'Not by might nor by power, but by my Spirit,' says the LORD Almighty.
(Zech 4v 6)

Jesus worked beautifully with what was already happening around Him. He reads the situation masterfully. It jars when we try to impose our agenda without nuance onto every situation. He doesn't say, 'I could do this in my sleep, I've dealt with women like her before, here goes'. Jesus doesn't have an appendix in His training manual for how to witness to immoral women. He flows with the Holy Spirit with excellent emotional intelligence.

It's so tempting to turn our 'successes' into formulae, it's a very human instinct, but it means our methods crystallise and become less and less effective. There is always movement in the activity of the Holy Spirit; symbolised by wind, water, fire, rain, river, streams etc. None of these forms stay still, there's a flow.

This flow can only come out of deep relationship and it challenges our human desire for formulae and rituals. We're rock climbing without safety harnesses! But when we experience it, we wonder why we ever do anything else. It's like surfing. There is a wave of the beautiful Holy Spirit that we can catch which will carry us through triumphantly. Holy Spirit does the work, He sets the direction. We simply jump onto the wave and let Him lead us at His speed and trajectory. Jesus makes it look effortlessly simple. It takes a lot of skill to do that!

Be purposeful without rushing

There's no sense of Jesus rushing to get to His big 'evangelistic' right-hook and to a commitment! He lets things gently unfold and the conversation to breathe, but never wastes a single word. Being economical with our words is a great skill. When we're feeling insecure some of us speak fast and fill the space with utter nonsense.

> *"you are worried and upset about many things, but few things are needed—or indeed only one'.*
> (Luke 10v 41b–42b)

Jesus is not afraid of being misunderstood by the woman, His disciples or the Samaritan villagers. His identity is in His Father. He is not anxious to justify Himself to anyone and therefore is not hurried. I might think, '*I've got to finish this before the others get back, otherwise there'll be ruffled feathers and dissension. I know what I'm doing but they'll never understand'*. If we are free from the fear of man we will be able to go at the pace of the Holy Spirit and not the dictates of our anxiety.

Resist distractions

I got into a meaningful conversation with a man in Norwich, he was sharing painful things in his life, and I offered to pray in Jesus' name for healing. He was open to this and was welling up. At this moment his companion who had been quiet until this point suddenly became very animated. He clumsily interrupted our conversation with a completely random train of thought. It was nothing to do with what we had been talking about, so was obviously 'spiritual interference'.

> *'Let the peace of Christ rule in your hearts, since as members of one body you were called to peace. And be thankful'.*
> (Col 3v 15)

I did pray in my mind to bind up confusion, but I was alone; it would have helped to have someone alongside in support. The confusion was such we never got back to where we were, I did pray briefly but the moment had passed. The enemy loves to throw confusion in and we need to be wise to this. We do not have to go down every conversational blind alley that we are led to. The antidote is to stay in the peace of God, then we can overcome confusion rather than be swept away with it. We get better at this the more practice we have.

An impossible standard?

We may never attain to the brilliance of Jesus in prophetic evangelism, but this is not a reason to discount ourselves. We must start somewhere. All heaven waits with bated breath for our decision to engage with God, be filled with the Holy Spirit so as to tell people about Jesus. God will certainly put the resources of heaven at our disposal if we once determine to do this. God only asks that we obey the call,

'Therefore, I urge you, brothers and sisters, in view of God's mercy, to offer your bodies as a living sacrifice, holy and pleasing to God – this is your true and proper worship'. (Romans 12v 1)

Part 4

*Prophetic
Evangelism
– practicalities*

13 *I'm no prophetic evangelist, how do I do this?*

Earlier we discussed the close connection between love and prophecy. Our starting point is that we want to bring people to a place of committing to Jesus and experiencing His forgiveness and love. God is love and love is always communicating and reproducing itself. God is continually speaking to His creation through His living Word, His Holy Spirit, His people and the natural world (Rev 14v 2).

The Word became flesh and made his dwelling among us. We have seen his glory, the glory of the one and only Son, who came from the Father, full of grace and truth.
(John 1v 14)

Some churches view evangelism nervously and adding the prophetic dimension on top of this can 'blow' their proverbial 'fuse'! They're not accustomed to expecting God to speak in anything but a general way and therefore do not look for such revelation.

Conversely some people's ecclesiology expects God to speak, even requires Him to. Prophets have particularly acute spiritual hearing (they are the ears of the body 1 Cor 12v 12), but everyone can hear God. Especially where it pertains to the lost, God is very generous in His communication, because He wants to reach them even more than we do. Realizing that God 'knows' them (re. Samaritan woman at the well) is sometimes all that is needed for broken people to give their lives to Him. We can all get better at hearing God, it's an invaluable skill. Experience only comes by doing. (Hebrews 5v 14)

There are some simple practical steps that we can take to improve our ability to hear God. It's not that God needs our help, but our lives can get very cluttered at times. Here we explore seven:

1. Short accounts with God

We can make sure there are no blockages. Obviously, we want to live close to God with very short accounts (i.e. virtually no time between conviction

Search me, God, and know my heart; test me and know my anxious thoughts. See if there is any offensive way in me, and lead me in the way everlasting.
(Psalm 139v 23-24)

and repentance) but sometimes things can sneak up on us. The big things we deal with, but it's the little stones in our shoes, that we only stop and take out when we've started running. It's always good practice and highly biblical to ask the Holy Spirit to search us. Let's not go fishing ourselves, if He doesn't show us anything let's move on.

2. De-clutter

We can intentionally de-clutter our minds and hearts, leaving our burdens with Him. Phones turned off! Cares and concerns can build up in our minds and hearts if we don't 'Cast all your anxiety on him because he cares for you'. (1 Peter 5v 7) It can be helpful to have soaking music or quiet worship. The prophets would often ask for a musician to come to facilitate their prophesying.

But now bring me a harpist." While the harpist was playing, the hand of the LORD came on Elisha
(2 Kings 3v 15)

3. Give God faith

We sincerely believe in our heads and hearts that God wants to speak to us. We don't have to fight for it or work for it. In Christ we are accepted and chosen. You might think that's a given, but we can have deep seated lies in our hearts that we've accepted about ourselves and God (we may not even be aware of them- they're called strongholds). For instance, if our significant authority figures never seemed to have time for us or bothered to communicate meaningfully with us we may project this onto God to some degree. As humans we are made in the image of God and all our relationships are designed to teach us something about the nature of God. When they are less than perfect, which relationships always are, they can alter our perception of God. We are all works in progress and God has grace for us, but we do bring some baggage with us, even if at an unconscious level. Always we should invite and welcome God's Holy Spirit to counsel, heal and instruct us (Genesis 18v 17, Matt 7v 11).

4. Get into the word

'Keep this Book of the Law always on your lips; meditate on it day and night, so that you may be careful to do everything written in it. Then you will be prosperous and successful'. (Josh 1v 8)

As we spend time meditating on the Bible we discover God's revealed will. It always enriches us but sometimes we hear in a very specific way. Other times it's after a period of study, maybe later in the day, that God will speak to us.

'And the words of the LORD are flawless, like silver purified in a crucible, like gold refined seven times'. (Psalm 12v 6)

We may become aware the Holy Spirit is drawing our attention to specific parts of the passage we are studying. There are simple exercises we can do, like asking God about which Bible character He wants us to inhabit as He speaks to us. He can show us what part of their life is relevant to us today, and how we should apply this. God is expert in taking our daily Bible readings and speaking through them as if we were the only ones they were prepared for. This is what we might call 'now' or rhema words (Prov 25v 11).

5. Cry out for the lost

We get God's attention straight away when we cry out for the lost. We can be bold in asking for words and impressions for them. 'Give us the nations for our inheritance Lord' (Psalm 2v 8). Evangelism is very close to God's heart. If we want to hear His heartbeat praying for the lost is a sure way of doing that. God will be only too happy to give us pointers.

> *'When he saw the crowds, he had compassion on them, because they were harassed and helpless, like sheep without a shepherd'.* (Matthew 9v 36)

Praying for the lost is so healthy, it opens a clear channel between us and God. Our prayer meetings can get inward looking and introspective. Bless me, bless him, bless my cat etc. As we put aside our personal struggles God goes to battle on our behalf. It might be that some fasting (which can take many forms, it's not exclusively food) can help us get God's heart for them,

> *'The Lord is not slow in keeping his promise, as some understand slowness. Instead he is patient with you, not wanting anyone to perish, but everyone to come to repentance'.* (2 Peter 3v 9)

6. Rest in God

It's counter-intuitive and a discipline for evangelists who are generally activists and 'doers' to take time in God's presence. We must give God time, and not try to rush Him. He's very good at saving people and has a long-range plan which won't be upset if we fail to knock doors in the next hour. Sometimes we can take silence as a 'non-answer' and feel intimidated by it. I can enjoy silence with my wife because we know each other well and are comfortable in each other's company. Some people who are nervous about silence blather on to cover it; it can be exhausting!

Silence can indicate that God has nothing new to say to us and we are on the right track. Or it can be a pregnant pause full of the Holy Spirit's brooding, followed by a 'God' thought/word/picture. If we're not willing to wait in God's presence (which is an end in itself) then we may never get to the point of hearing something. We tell our secrets to those who will invest time and listen to us properly.

> *'After the earthquake came a fire, but the LORD was not in the fire. And after the fire came a gentle whisper'.* (1 Kings 19v 12)

7. Practical and spiritual input

We shouldn't dismiss thoughts if they are not obviously spiritual. I used to think that when I daydreamed in prayer meetings this was undisciplined of me– 'couldn't you watch with me even one hour?'(Matt 26v 40 NLT) But now I trust that God is working through my sanctified imagination, sifting through my memories and plans and depositing something of His wisdom in me. I'm dreaming His dreams. God is practical as well, he might remind us of things we need to print off, or where we're going to find the most footfall in the town.

What happens next?

'Information/Revelation/Evaluation/Interpretation/Application'

These suggestions are not formulas to be applied 'religiously'. Our readiness and desire to listen to God is like digging a hole in a sandy beach. Sooner or later the tide will turn and bring huge volumes of water over that hole, which will then fill up. The water represents the Holy Spirit and the Word of God. After the tide has ebbed the hole will remain full of water because we've done the hard work in advance. It's a difficult tension, if we don't position ourselves to hear from God we may not notice when He speaks. We're royal sons and daughters, and as such are entitled to hear from our Father and King. But by the same token He does honour and invest Himself in our preparation. Let's remember that as we welcome and honour the prophetic, we will receive more of it (Matthew 10v 41).

> *'And without faith it is impossible to please God, because anyone who comes to him must believe that he exists and that he rewards those who earnestly seek him'.*
> (Hebrews 11v 6)

There are general tools for 'processing' prophecy. Receiving from God is all about relationship, however there are pointers that can help us. These five stages can help us to stand back from what we've heard and objectify a little bit:

1. Information

What are the facts? What is the context? Someone presents with severe disability and depression, or there's a part of town where knife crime and prostitution are rampant, how do we take the gospel there?

2. Revelation

Receiving directly from God. This is deeply personal and flows out of our relationship with Jesus. There's an aspect of this that can't be taught, it has to be 'caught'. There's simply no substitute for developing a personal 'love language' with Jesus. Where God is wanted and welcomed He will make His habitation. As we develop deep friendship with Jesus, His Spirit will presence Himself with us. ***Worship God! For it is the Spirit of prophecy who bears testimony to Jesus."*** (Rev 19v 10b)

3. Evaluation

Did I add anything, or take anything away? Am I projecting my desires? Needs? How stable/ peaceful was I when I heard from God. Am I hearing my own heart? Does it line up with the general will of God revealed in Scripture? God will never contradict His own Word. Not paralysis by analysis but sober evaluation. Is this something I need to share discreetly with my team leader? God will speak to the leader if anything should be done about it. (1 Cor 14v 29)

4. Interpretation

This needs as much care as hearing God. We can think we've got the right interpretation and yet get it badly wrong. There's wisdom in sharing with our leader and teams. Timings need prayer; has God shown us something that has happened or is it for now, later, or the distant future?

5. Application

This also needs much weighing in prayer. It is the practical outworking of the revelation we've received. Is it for praying/sharing/doing? Every time it can be different. For example God might be saying 'that district of town is dangerous, there's gang activity'. This could mean, don't ever go there, pray before you go, wait until you can go in larger numbers, or several other interpretations! If there's no clear interpretation revelation can bring doubt, confusion and even division. We mustn't assume that as soon as we have received revelation 'we can take it from here, thanks God'. That's why these general tools for processing direct revelation can be so helpful.

'Where there is no revelation, people cast off restraint; but blessed is the one who heeds wisdom's instruction'. (Prov 29v 18)

14 *Up, down, in, out!*

Following directly from chapter 13, a different way of looking at the same process of receiving revelation can be helpfully guided by our motifs; up, down, in and out!

UP we reach up to God in worship, adoration, gratitude and prayerful expectation. We yield our hearts to Him and kiss the Son, lest He be angry (Psalm 2v 12). We fix our eyes upon Him, the author and perfecter of our faith (Hebrews 12v 2). We lift up Holy hands in worship and pray His Kingdom come and His Will be done. We cry out for the last, the lost and the least.

DOWN as we send up the vapour of our love and worship He sends the 'rain' of His word and presence (Joel 2 v23). As we reach towards Him, He releases his beautiful Spirit to come and minister to us. Often in these moments we receive pictures, impressions and words.

IN we take His words, pictures and impressions and weigh them in our hearts. What are You saying Lord, what do You want me to do with the revelation You have given me? Like Mary who pondered these things in her heart (Luke 2v 19).

OUT in faith we step out on the water of God's Word. Like Peter we trust that God has spoken and His Word is what holds the Universe together. We 'walk' on the words God has given us (Matt 14v 29). We share them as He leads and guides us, according to our level of faith, experience and gifting.

We want to use prophecy biblically and pastorally. We have options in front of us, once we're sure we've heard from God. We don't have to blurt it straight out. We might ask, is what we have heard for ...name...?

Sharing?

Some things that God tells us are obviously for sharing, and it would be wrong of us not to. If, for instance, we sense God is saying tell that person 'I love them and I'm looking after their family', they need us to open our mouths and tell them. Love not expressed is love not received.

If what we have to share is in a church context, for instance on a Sunday morning some churches have a protocol to run it past the pastor or leader and he or she will indicate whether it is appropriate to share. Accountability is a good and biblical principle that we should welcome (Eph 5v 21).

I did a whole day of teaching about prophetic protocol once. I laboured the point that giving prophetic predictions on marriages, babies and deaths are for those who are experienced with a recognised prophetic gift, and even then it should be done with pastoral sensitivity. One man came forward and launched into a prediction over my wife and I about us having a baby girl. At the time the whole subject was very painful for us. I chose to smile rather than cry as I wondered how little impact the teaching can have had on him. He was right though.

Praying?

We mustn't assume that everything God tells us is for immediate sharing. Sometimes it will be for prayer. I mentioned previously my efforts to be available to God on public transport. Sometimes I have felt he showed me some information about the person opposite or next to me. For example one lady was very unhappy and her marriage was on the rocks. Would it be appropriate to lean across and tell her this? Probably not (unless God was very strongly saying otherwise). It's safe to say this information is for praying. Unless we got into an amazing conversation this information would be a juggernaut to drive across a non-existent relational bridge. So I prayed protection for her children (she was speaking to them on the phone) and healing for her marriage. God wasn't expecting me to do anything else but pray. Prayer is not a 'soft' option.

'For the revelation awaits
an appointed time;'
(Habakkuk 2v 3)

For holding before God?

Some things are for sharing but not immediately. Revelation can be time sensitive. If we share it at the wrong moment it will be received negatively but at the right moment it will bring great blessing and release faith.

For giving to authority figures?

We may be uncertain about what we should do with some revelation. Some information might be humiliating just to pour it out. A good acid test would be how would I like it if someone brought this 'word' to me (Matt 7v 12)? God has given us leaders and/or mentors to help us when we are not sure how to proceed. They can steer us away from classic mistakes in handling revelation. For instance we must be very cautious in bringing directive words; never tell someone to throw away their medication!

Afterwards we let go of it .... we've done our bit

When God has spoken to us, it is a very precious thing and it's right we feel the gravitas of it. It's hard when people don't react with what we would consider the appropriate level of enthusiasm or interest. Paul instructed the Thessalonians 'not to despise' prophecy because he knew there was a very present temptation to do so. A reaction might be it's just old so and so banging their drum again! If we sense this attitude it is tempting to keep hold of our 'word' and keep agitating until we get the reaction we want. We may, in frustration, 'add' to it but this is totally counterproductive.

Pastors can be wary of prophecy because they know that some people will keep pushing an agenda afterwards. In my days of pastoring a group brought me a 'word' that came with huge pressure attached to it from them, an ultimatum really. I refused to receive it. Firstly I didn't think God would speak like that and secondly, even if He had, it wasn't so as to manipulate me. All that is required of us is to appropriately pass on what God has shown us and leave it there (Ezekiel 33v 4-5).

A picture of prophetic evangelism

I find it helpful to picture myself as an eagle soaring high on Holy Spirit thermals and scanning the land below. I pray *Lord show me what you want me to see.* Eagles have exceptional eyesight, on average five times better vision than humans. Their eyes are designed to be able to focus on small objects that are very far away and are much bigger proportionally to their head size than human eyes. An eagle can see for miles, and swoop on its 'prey' with stunning speed and silence. Animals on the ground know that if they've been spotted by an eagle their days are numbered. We do not swoop on people to kill them, but to share the gospel with them.

In prophetic evangelism, rather like an eagle, we are lifted above the tyranny of the urgent and the seething masses to a quiet place. Here God shows us one person with a heart that is searching for Jesus, or whatever the scenario may be. The Ethiopian eunuch was brought to the attention of the evangelist Philip in such a way (Acts 8). Who does God want to draw your attention to?

I stood in a crowded carriage on the Piccadilly line. Most of us had just come on board from King's Cross. As I glanced down the train I saw a dignified man and did a double take, it couldn't be? It was, a famous sportsman whom I regularly saw on TV. He had been famous in the Christian world as well but recently there were magazine articles about him turning away from his Christian faith amongst other things.

Without any conscious thought I moved towards him, staggering past commuters on a busy train and trying to keep my composure. With every step closer to him my heart rose into my mouth. My head felt like it was throbbing visibly. I drew his attention by moving into his space, how do you broach a conversation naturally in these settings?

'Could I take a moment of your time' I coughed. He inclined his head slightly. I sputtered out a short message that I felt God was giving me for him. He didn't flinch as I searched his inscrutable face for a reaction. *'Thanks for your time'* I said with every ounce of breeziness I could muster and turned away, wishing with every fibre of my being to arrive at the station so I could vanish into the crowds. I could feel my neck burning, was he staring angrily at me from behind? Who did I think I was walking up to him just like that? As I rapidly disembarked there was a breeze behind me and a tap on the shoulder. He said *'well done, it takes a lot of courage to do that'* and with a waft of expensive cologne he was gone.

15 *Four voices*

As we set ourselves to hear God we can rest assured He will speak, and patiently teach us how to listen for His voice. But it is worth remembering that there are other voices that may clamour for our attention. I cannot emphasize enough the importance of immersing ourselves in the Word of God. If we get the Bible flowing in our spiritual bloodstream we have immunity from many deceptive viruses (Matt 24v 11). Here we reflect briefly on four competing voices between which we must distinguish:

> *'If any of you lacks wisdom, you should ask God, who gives generously to all without finding fault, and it will be given to you. But when you ask, you must believe and not doubt, because the one who doubts is like a wave of the sea, blown and tossed by the wind'.*
> (James 1v 5-6)

1. God's voice

There's nothing more precious than hearing God's voice.
There is no short cut to this, there may be times God needs to get through to us and He 'shouts' but for the day to day hearing, it's a long walk holding Jesus' hand listening for His familiar voice (Gen 5v 22). This takes time, commitment to intimacy and long term communion with Him; spending time with no agendas. Perhaps it's more a case of we know it when we hear it. As we hear and obey His voice our confidence develops, the relationship deepens and trust flourishes. Even our mistakes lead us back to Him, there is delight in reaching out to a God who runs to us. (Luke 15v 11-32).

2. Our own hearts

Our own hearts/flesh can get excited when the Holy Spirit is moving, yet be deceived. Our human compassion and sympathy can masquerade as the kindness of God but they have no redemptive power, and can actually perpetuate sin. Giving money to an homeless addict (every situation is different) might seem right, but can facilitate something that is deeply sinful. Our heart may speak and we're confused thinking it was God.

Human kindness and goodwill cannot save anyone, otherwise the cross would not have been necessary. As harsh as this may sound, we must keep our human desire to make everything better in check. Jesus passed by a lot of sick people and dysfunctional situations, He addressed only those the Father showed Him. Succumbing to human sympathy could have wrecked Jesus' mission more surely then direct attacks from the devil.

Our 'good' hearts are prone to do the right thing for the wrong reasons, or the wrong thing for the right reasons. We want to bless what God has judged and judge someone that God is merciful towards. We mustn't uncritically follow our hearts, they can be wander off track. The good is often the enemy of the best! Our hearts can 'hear' good ideas and seek to fulfil desires which interfere with, or even undermine, God's best (this is humanism!). Christians who do this end up in some very compromised and unbiblical scenarios. Just because it feels right doesn't mean it is right!

3. The devil

He is most dangerous when he comes as an angel of light (2 Corinthians 11v 14). The deeper our relationship goes with God, the subtler the enemy is in seeking to deceive us. He can be quite blatant with someone who doesn't know God, but he must work harder with someone who has God's Word in his heart and a living friendship with Him. He is the father of lies (John 8v 44) and our protection against his devious deception is feeding on God's truth. He will question what God is saying especially when he knows our desires (Gen 3v 1) but He is also an impersonator (Matt 4v 9). Our only safety is to live in God's presence; feasting continually on His word, bringing everything into His light.

'I have hidden your word in my heart that I might not sin against you'.
(Psalm 119v 11)

4. Others people's hearts.

If we are prophetic and empathic we can pick up on what someone else's heart is saying, intuiting their desires and longings. I knew of someone who had been picked out with her husband in large Christian meetings three times on separate occasions and in different places to be told she would have children. This was the desperate longing of her heart but it never happened, at least not as she would have wanted. She had three miscarriages which as you can imagine was desperately painful, compounded by the fact this seemed to go against what God had spoken. I still have questions about situations like this where prophecy seems to do the opposite of comfort, edify and encourage. The only thing we can do is go back to God with our raw pain and confusion.

Could it be that the 'prophets' were picking up on her heart? Were they prophesying her will as if it was God's, because of their kind hearts? We don't understand everything. We see through a glass darkly, (1 Cor 13v 12). That's the challenge of prophecy and why we need to handle it with humility and pastoral wisdom.

Someone wise said, *'when we are in a situation where we can evangelise, it's likely the first voice we hear is God. The second voice is our own and then the enemy trying to stop us altogether with the third voice'.*

Here's a hypothetical example where we encounter three voices: I come bouncing out of the morning prayer meeting feeling full of God and glad to be alive! Watch out world I hum quietly, as I go about my jobs. I'm in the local supermarket and feel strangely drawn to a particular person. Then a glistening thought pierces my thoughts, *'I want you to pay for that man's groceries and tell him I'm going to help him with his debts'.* Hot on the heels of this first thought come others. *'I can't do that, he'd be insulted if I offered, and anyway I'm behind budget this month myself. He's got nice clothes on, and it looks like he's financially well off. He's leaving now anyway, I'll say a prayer for him instead. If I ever see him again then I'll definitely do something'.* Now I am seriously wavering; hesitation is fatal in this type of situation.

Then there is a third and unpleasant voice, the enemy ups the ante. *'They'll think you're ridiculous if you do this, it's just your wandering thoughts you're listening to. It's your need to be the hero with the grand gesture, it's pathetic. This is all about you, not him. Why don't you sort your own life out before you start meddling with other peoples?'*

Forgive me laying it on thick but these outcomes highlight whether we evangelise depending on which voice we listen to. You might think it extreme, but these voices influence all of us, possibly more than we would care to admit.

Immediate obedience to the first voice

With a thudding heart I sidle up to the man, striking while the iron is hot. I don't allow any time between hearing the voice and obeying it. Clearing my throat I try to spark up a conversation and build a bridge. I make a comment about the weather. *'Listen mate, this is going to sound really strange. I'm a Christian, I don't know if that means anything to you? I want to pay for your groceries. Would you be willing to let me do that for you?'*

The man's mouth opens and flaps in the wind. Finally he croaks, *'This is absolutely incredible, incredible. I'm in financial 'do do'. I've only just got enough left on my credit card overdraft to pay for this lot (pointing at the groceries). I'm looking at eviction from my flat and my job may or may not be there for me at the end of the summer. The strangest thing is last week I was feeling so desperate, I said into thin air, 'God if you're there, prove it to me by helping me with my debt'. 'My Granny was a religious person you see', he offered apologetically, 'does that seem weird?'*

After paying for the groceries and on the way out to the car I continue, *'Jack (we're on first name terms now) God wants to tell you that this little of bit of help today is a sign to you of bigger help on the way for your debts. There's an organisation called CAP that have a drop-in on Thursday in the town'.*

'I'll take all the help I can take', says Jack. 'In that case here's my number and if you text me I'll send you the details for CAP' I reply. In fact, can I pray for you right now. Then and there in the carpark I pray for Jack, who is visibly moved and holding back tears. I drive off, exhilarated to have had such a big impact on his life and decide I'm going to pray for him every day now. I can't wait to tell my wife what has happened. Next time, I conclude, I'm always going to listen to that first voice. I'd rather be wrong and look an idiot than miss what God is doing.

Delayed obedience after listening to the second voice

I'm in the local supermarket; right there in the home-baking aisle a battle is raging in my mind! The second thoughts have completely confused the first. I am paralysed by indecision, the moment is slipping by. I smile at the man as he walks past and make a comment about the weather. I've blown it now, I think, I can't go chasing after him.

I'll say a prayer for him, I think hollowly. I decide to get my small group praying for him when we next meet, omitting to mention the full message that I originally got from God. If I see him around town I'll know I should speak to him, and if that happens, I won't miss my opportunity. I pray for him again as I leave the shop. I'm deflated after this experience and take a couple of hours to shake off the feeling of having been a bit of a coward. A few weeks later I see him drive past but there is no opportunity to speak. His circumstances change and he moves away.

Listening to the third voice

The devil who has pressured me into passive torpor now pounds my mind with condemnation. His twin weapons of fear then condemnation are very effective. I stand staring at the eggs unseeing. A heaviness creeps over me. *'Isn't God fortunate to have such a coward in his army. You'll never amount to anything, God would be better off without you. You're only a Christian when you're with your Christian friends; everywhere else you just go with the flow like everyone else.'*

'Why am I so useless? I prayed this morning that I wanted courage to tell people about Jesus. I wish I hadn't now because I feel so defeated. I think I need to stop praying things that I don't really mean, there's nothing worse than a hypocrite. I feel strangely annoyed by the man because he becomes the focus of my 'failure'. I don't pray all day because I'm sure God must be disappointed. I'll leave this evangelism lark for those that have got a spine, unlike me.'

To some extent these three outcomes all depend on who we listen to. It boils down to this, we have to trust God's ability to lead us is greater than the devil's plan to deceive us; or our own capacity to confuse ourselves. Even if we get our listening bit wrong God is so pleased that we want to tell people about Jesus that he blesses it anyway.

The fourth voice

Let's take a different scenario for this one: George has severe cancer which had now metastasised to all his major organs. Sara, a Christian who is passionate about healing ministry visits George and his wife Patricia in hospital. Sara has a good track record of hearing from God, she is well intentioned and full of faith. She quickly picks up on Patricia's heart, which is desperate for George to survive, and George's. He wants to live for his wife's sake and to see his grandchildren born.

Sara being very prophetic absorbs all of this very naturally and spiritualises it. She confidently proclaims, 'God is going to heal you within the month and everyone will give glory to God'. In a general sense God is the healer and He does want to heal but Sara is mistaking what she's hearing from Patricia's heart for God's voice. Everyone is delighted with what Sara shares, it's just what they wanted to hear, further confirming in her mind that this is of God and it's just a case of waiting for the healing to manifest.

One month later, earlier than the doctors had predicted, George dies at home. Patricia is devastated, she had pinned all her hopes on George being healed. He didn't have the opportunity to say goodbye to his children or welcome his first grandchild. She now must wrestle with uncomfortable feelings about being deceived by God alongside crushing grief.

Sara never visits Patricia after George's death or mentions it again.

Although what she said in the hospital was within God's general will, she hadn't heard from God on this occasion. She listened to their hearts. Tragically the result is pain, confusion and loss of faith. All from a very good and genuine desire to see God heal.

This scenario is in no way meant to discourage healing prayer and I believe absolutely God can and does heal, often alongside prophetic insight. What it does show us is how easy it is to confuse the voices we're hearing when we are emotionally involved. Naturally, we have a human desire to bring hope and a Godly desire to speak faith. Often, we don't understand why God does heal in one instance and not in another, but we persist in faith, refusing to reduce our theology to the level of our experience and understanding.

If we're going to grow we have to take risks and there is grace in God but we aim to distinguish God's voice above all the others. In the next chapter we will see how some of the best prophetic evangelists in the New Testament learnt how to do this on the job. We can take encouragement from Peter, Philip and Paul who all needed lots of help. They give us permission to try our prophetic evangelist wings. Just like the mother eagle, God knows exactly when we are ready to be pushed out of the nest to try our wings and discover we can fly for ourselves.

A true story of listening to the fourth voice

A friend told me of his church where a good Christian man was very seriously ill – he hovered between life and death for some weeks. Earnestly his church (and perhaps others, too) prayed for life and for complete healing. But the prayers went unanswered; neither life nor death was given. Eventually his church prayed that God's perfect Will would be done and they returned the man to God's tender care. Within twenty-four hours he slipped peacefully away from this mortal world and into his Father's immediate presence!

Sometimes, with good intentions, we can pray for the wrong thing. We have to listen out for the Spirit's clear prompting. At the risk of stating the obvious, the "death" of a true Christian is never a tragedy, it is always a triumph and a transformation. (Psalm 116 v 15)

16 Peter, Philip and Paul – prophetic evangelists

'About noon the following day as they were on their journey and approaching the city, Peter went up on the roof to pray. He became hungry and wanted something to eat, and while the meal was being prepared, he fell into a trance. He saw heaven opened and something like a large sheet being let down to earth by its four corners. It contained all kinds of four-footed animals, as well as reptiles and birds. Then a voice told him, "Get up, Peter. Kill and eat."

"Surely not, Lord!" Peter replied. "I have never eaten anything impure or unclean."

The voice spoke to him a second time, "Do not call anything impure that God has made clean."

This happened three times, and immediately the sheet was taken back to heaven.

While Peter was wondering about the meaning of the vision, the men sent by Cornelius found out where Simon's house was and stopped at the gate. They called out, asking if Simon who was known as Peter was staying there.

While Peter was still thinking about the vision, the Spirit said to him, "Simon, three men are looking for you. So get up and go downstairs. Do not hesitate to go with them, for I have sent them."

Peter went down and said to the men, "I'm the one you're looking for. Why have you come?" (Acts 10v 9-21)

Peter, Philip and Paul each had powerful evangelistic ministries. In the book of Acts we see clearly how they are prophetically guided in these. Their mandate is enormous, the task is so overwhelming and dangers so omnipresent they need help in strategy. Prophetic evangelism hangs on being in the right place at the right time with God. This began to happen almost as 'second nature' as they obeyed God.

In Peter's ministry we watch with bated breath as he is temporarily seconded by the Holy Spirit from his apostleship to the Jews to visit a spiritually searching Gentile centurion. This is a big departure for the Galilean Peter in cultural understanding and ministry focus. In this passage for the third time recorded in scripture Peter insists, 'Surely not Lord'(John 13v 8, Matt 16v 22) . He is given a vision and clear instructions from the Holy Spirit as he is given an assignment that would be cultural anathema to him.

If Peter had not been open to prophetic guidance he would not have made this extremely fruitful short term mission trip. His evangelism to the Centurion and his household carries a strong prophetic edge, immediately slicing through layers of culture, history and prejudice. We will find that God does the same with us if we allow him, like Peter we'll be catching up with what He is doing, and loving it:

Then Peter said, "Surely no one can stand in the way of their being baptized with water. They have received the Holy Spirit just as we have." (Acts 10 v 46–47)

Prophetic direction in ministry

'The Spirit of the Sovereign LORD is on me, because the LORD has anointed me to proclaim good news to the poor. He has sent me to bind up the broken-hearted, to proclaim freedom for the captives and release from darkness for the prisoners.' (Isa 61v 1)

Although I don't for a minute compare myself with Peter, Philip or Paul, the Holy Spirit has guided my ministry prophetically just as he did for them. You can expect the same!

Gerald Coates (founder of the Pioneer Christian Network) came to our training block. The atmosphere in the room was electric, expectation hanging thick in the air, he had a reputation as a prophet. This was my second year of discipleship training , the first year at this same point I was desperate to get a 'word' from the Lord through Gerald. This time round I was more philosophical about it, hopefully this was a bit of maturity seeping in, I was happy to see the year one students being prophesied over. I concluded that if God needed to get a message to me he could do it very easily through any number of people.

So, I was surprised when I was picked out and asked to stand up. My heart starting chugging like a stream train. Two people either side stepped in to hold me up by my arms. It was like being plugged into the national grid, surges of Holy Spirit power saturated my body, my spirit was standing up on stilts, every cell in my body responded enthusiastically to the living Word of God. Gerald prophesied over me that I would play a big part of the healing of the nations, (Rev 22) and God was anointing me in the healing ministry, especially with the mentally ill, depressed and outcast. I would bring the Kingdom of God wherever I went and what I had seen so far was just the beginning. The flow of the Holy Spirit was going to get stronger, wider and deeper in my ministry, like the river that flows out of God's temple (Ezek 47).

These were all things that I had sensed in my spirit, although I'd not articulated them out loud. It's strange how encouraging it is to be told something we already know. Gerald didn't know that I was working part time at this time as a mental health recovery worker (alongside being assistant pastor) and was being stirred up by the Holy Spirit in missions. Being recognised by God through a gifted prophetic person is incredibly life-affirming. It's powerful to be publicly recognised and endorsed in your calling. My confidence certainly increased, discouragements from the past were broken off me. This prophecy gave me more shape and purpose as I was encouraged that my ministry emphasis was correct.

From this point on there was a noticeable shift and increase of anointing in my life and ministry, my confidence skyrocketed. Within two weeks I had led someone suffering with quite severe mental health issues to Christ.

Philip the prophetic evangelist

Philip is the only person in the Bible called an evangelist (Acts 21v 8), and not for no reason, he led a very successful evangelistic campaign in the city of Samaria, signs and wonders were flowing. His preaching was listened to and highly impacting. Perhaps we would have said he should stay there and carry on the good work. But God had other ideas about what should happen, there was someone for him to meet. Acts is so full of the supernatural that we hardly blink at an angel telling Philip about a new assignment.

Now an angel of the Lord said to Philip, "Go south to the road—the desert road—that goes down from Jerusalem to Gaza." So he started out, and on his way he met an Ethiopian

'Those who had been scattered preached the word wherever they went. Philip went down to a city in Samaria and proclaimed the Messiah there. When the crowds heard Philip and saw the signs he performed, they all paid close attention to what he said. For with shrieks, impure spirits came out of many, and many who were paralyzed or lame were healed. So there was great joy in that city'.
(Acts 8v 4–8)

eunuch, an important official in charge of all the treasury of the Kandake (which means "queen of the Ethiopians"). This man had gone to Jerusalem to worship, and on his way home was sitting in his chariot reading the Book of Isaiah the prophet. The Spirit told Philip, "Go to that chariot and stay near it."

Then Philip ran up to the chariot and heard the man reading Isaiah the prophet. "Do you understand what you are reading?" Philip asked. "How can I," he said, "unless someone explains it to me?" So he invited Philip to come up and sit with him. This is the passage of Scripture the eunuch was reading:

> *"He was led like a sheep to the slaughter,*
> *and as a lamb before its shearer is silent,*
> *so he did not open his mouth.*
>
> *In his humiliation he was deprived of justice.*
> *Who can speak of his descendants?*
> *For his life was taken from the earth."*

The eunuch asked Philip, "Tell me, please, who is the prophet talking about, himself or someone else?" Then Philip began with that very passage of Scripture and told him the good news about Jesus. As they travelled along the road, they came to some water and the eunuch said, "Look, here is water. What can stand in the way of my being baptised?" And he gave orders to stop the chariot. Then both Philip and the eunuch went down into the water and Philip baptised him. When they came up out of the water, the Spirit of the Lord suddenly took Philip away, and the eunuch did not see him again, but went on his way rejoicing. Philip, however, appeared at Azotus and travelled about, preaching the gospel in all the towns until he reached Caesarea. (Acts 8v 26–41)

Philip moves from a prophetic dream scenario to a real physical encounter. From a city-wide Samaritan revival with its continual healings and deliverance, to an influential man reading Isaiah 53 (perhaps the most Christ-centric prophetic chapter in the entire Bible) and needing an explanation. Philip is served up two golden evangelistic platters in the space of one chapter!

But imagine if he had not been willing to listen to or obey the angel's message. He dropped everything, left the big evangelistic platform in Samaria, trusted God to look after the revival and went to do His bidding. I wonder how many of us would have dug our heels in and refused to leave something that was so outwardly successful. We can so easily think that God needs us to finish a task in which He generously included us, at its beginning. In the Kingdom of God the best way to keep hold of something is to give it away.

In the parable of the good shepherd, Jesus leaves the ninety nine to go in search for the one lost sheep. Philip was a prophetic evangelist, willing to be supernaturally directed to the right place at the right time. Possibly the impact of this eunuch giving his life to Jesus would be greater as he returned to his homeland and his queen, than all the conversions in Samaria. We are not equipped to judge the impact or value of our actions, our simple obedience is the stone thrown into a lake – and where the ripples end up is not for us to know.

India– Overseas mission

My pastor at the time suggested I might like to try some overseas mission. She had been at a conference at which Jonathan Conrathe (Mission 24) was speaking and recommended I go with one of his teams. I liked this idea very much. As I investigated the options for the next year, 2013, there were short term missions in Africa or India. As I prayed I knew that I should go to India.

'To humans belong the plans of the heart, but from the LORD comes the proper answer of the tongue'. (Prov 16v 1)

My first dabble in overseas mission was not auspicious. Several days before departure from Gatwick I came down with a horrible bug. A very long overnight flight didn't help matters much and I arrived in Hyderabad looking and feeling like death warmed up. I dragged myself through the week having to spend two days lying in the hotel bed. It all seemed such a waste of time and money. It's dangerous to make judgements about this, only God knows, but it wasn't a cheap trip by any means. I felt like a drag on the team and was gutted to be so restricted in such an exciting place. I could have stayed at home and been sick in my own bed for free. On the Sunday, although streaming with a horrible cold, I was due to preach at one of the churches in Hyderabad that had been hosting the conference.

At the very last minute there was a switch around and I was sent to Pastor Moses and Nissi Faith Church in Kukatpally, Hyderabad. Although I was a long way from my best, I hit it off immediately with Pastor Moses. I preached my heart out and connected with his congregation too, a very spiritual group. Since then I have been out to visit him in Hyderabad three more times, and he's stayed with us twice. This is not to mention all the online contact back and forth and fundraising I've done for his orphanage. Only God knows what the full fruit of His 'light touch' guidance will be. This Kingdom friendship all stemmed from a last minute switch, as somebody was hearing God clearly. Big things can hinge on seemingly inconsequential decisions. I could have gone to another church and none of this would have happened. God knows how to direct us, even despite ourselves, in our frailty His glory is displayed! (2 Corinthians 12v 7-10) Destiny calls when we least expect it.

Paul's first missionary journey

Paul's is one of the most dramatic conversion experiences in the Bible, or possibly of all time. On the road to Damascus, breathing out murderous threats, Paul was pursuing the early 'followers of the Way' in order to persecute them. The risen Christ met him on the way, blinded him, bent his knees and showed him 'how much he must suffer for my name'.

To say Paul had a large ministry would be a massive understatement, he was the apostle to the Gentiles. The hugeness of it, the Gentile world, would paralyse most of us. Where do we even start? The way Paul strategized this evangelistic ministry to the Greek speaking world was very prophetic.

'Now in the church at Antioch there were prophets and teachers: Barnabas, Simeon called Niger, Lucius of Cyrene, Manaen (who had been brought up with Herod the tetrarch) and Saul. While they were worshipping the Lord and fasting, the Holy Spirit said, "Set apart for me Barnabas and Saul for the work to which I have called them."So after they had fasted and prayed, they placed their hands on them and sent them off. (Acts 13v 1-3)

This is the work of the prophetic ministry, to release people in a timely way into their call and destiny. Paul's ministry, which started with a prophetic edge, continued with one. As if it wasn't enough that he was 'sent out' by the prophets and teachers, this is underscored by *'The two of them, sent on their way by the Holy Spirit.'* (Acts 13v 4)

It is not unreasonable to assume that they had some prophetic 'direction' with this sending as to where they were to go and what they were to do. Paul and Barnabus minister with great effect through Cyprus (we know there were Cypriot Jews at Pentecost) and then all the way through Pisidian Antioch. As they worked round and spent some time in Iconium they avoided a trap to 'mistreat and stone them'. We are not explicitly told, but it could be they received a Holy Spirit warning to clear out.

Paul's second missionary journey

'Paul and his companions travelled throughout the region of Phrygia and Galatia, having been kept by the Holy Spirit from preaching the word in the

province of Asia. When they came to the border of Mysia, they tried to enter Bithynia, but the Spirit of Jesus would not allow them to. So they passed by Mysia and went down to Troas. During the night Paul had a vision of a man of Macedonia standing and begging him, "Come over to Macedonia and help us." After Paul had seen the vision, we got ready at once to leave for Macedonia, concluding that God had called us to preach the gospel to them'. (Acts 16v 6–10)

The launch point for Paul's second missionary experience is a prophetic experience. He is prevented by the Spirit from entering Bithynia because he is needed in Macedonia. God is not in the business of blocking us, without putting more fruitful work to our hands. It is clear guidance from God which elicits immediate obedient action from Paul. I wonder whether he was seeing a Macedonian actually in prayer, crying out at that moment for God's help and instruction? Either way, the sense conveyed is that they depart with urgency.

Paul's third missionary journey

One night the Lord spoke to Paul in a vision: "Do not be afraid; keep on speaking, do not be silent. For I am with you, and no one is going to attack and harm you, because I have many people in this city." So Paul stayed in Corinth for a year and a half, teaching them the word of God. (Acts 18v 9–11)

Sometimes the prophetic ministry moves us on and on other occasions it keeps us somewhere we'd otherwise leave. God knows where ministry will be most fruitful and His timing is perfect. Always God's Spirit searches for hearts that will receive the gospel (1 Cor 2v 10).

'There is a time for everything, and a season for every activity under the heavens:' (Eccles 3v 1)

Paul's final trip to Rome

'After we had been there a number of days, a prophet named Agabus came down from Judea. Coming over to us, he took Paul's belt, tied his own hands and feet with it and said, "The Holy Spirit says, 'In this way the Jewish leaders in Jerusalem will bind the owner of this belt and will hand him over to the Gentiles.'" (Acts 21v 10–11)

No one disputes that this revelation is from God but clearly Paul differs from the other leaders in how he applies it. He already knows what is awaiting him in Jerusalem, whereas they see it as a reason to turn back, this is what their hearts want anyway. Perhaps they were not in an objective place to process revelation from God. Paul had been shown at the inception of his apostolic ministry what he would suffer for Christ. The others did not have this experience and wanted to keep Paul with them. There are echoes in this of Peter telling Jesus he wouldn't allow him to go to Jerusalem (Matt 16v 22).

There is something undeniably special about the book of Acts and the beginning of the church. The Holy Spirit guidance is strong, unmistakable and supernatural. Maybe we won't be getting this level of guidance when we go out with our group for high street evangelism on Saturday morning. However, God is still speaking, we'll discover this if we are listening. Our passion for Jesus and for the lost must be given focus and shape, otherwise it's just lots of hot air and activity. As we engage in evangelism with prophetic direction from God, our efforts are fruitful. The precious seed of the gospel finds good soil and is not wasted.

'Be very careful, then, how you live—not as unwise but as wise, making the most of every opportunity, because the days are evil. Therefore do not be foolish, but understand what the Lord's will is'. (Eph 5v 15–17).

17 Prophetic evangelism in the End Times

'I was given a reed like a measuring rod and was told, "Go and measure the temple of God and the altar, with its worshippers. But exclude the outer court; do not measure it, because it has been given to the Gentiles. They will trample on the holy city for 42 months. And I will appoint my two witnesses, and they will prophesy for 1,260 days, clothed in sackcloth." They are "the two olive trees" and the two lampstands, and "they stand before the Lord of the earth." If anyone tries to harm them, fire comes from their mouths and devours their enemies. This is how anyone who wants to harm them must die. They have power to shut up the heavens so that it will not rain during the time they are prophesying; and they have power to turn the waters into blood and to strike the earth with every kind of plague as often as they want.

Now when they have finished their testimony, the beast that comes up from the Abyss will attack them, and overpower and kill them. Their bodies will lie in the public square of the great city—which is figuratively called Sodom and Egypt—where also their Lord was crucified. For three and a half days some from every people, tribe, language and nation will gaze on their bodies and refuse them burial. The inhabitants of the earth will gloat over them and will celebrate by sending each other gifts, because these two prophets had tormented those who live on the earth. But after the three and a half days the breath of life from God entered them, and they stood on their feet, and terror struck those who saw them. Then they heard a loud voice from heaven saying to them, "Come up here." And they went up to heaven in a cloud, while their enemies looked on. At that very hour there was a severe earthquake and a tenth of the city collapsed. Seven thousand people were killed in the earthquake, and the survivors were terrified and gave glory to the God of heaven. (Rev 11v 1–13)

This chapter makes no pretension of being a full exegesis of Revelation chapter 11. That prophetic book, Revelation - the New

Testament's only prophetic book - is presented in highly symbolic and apocalyptic language. Potentially there are as many interpretations of Revelation as there are people that study it. I intend, simply, to draw out some principles from it that pertain to our topic.

The measuring rod

God is always 'measuring', i.e. testing and evaluating His people, their level of maturity and obedience. We are given the same symbolic picture in Ezekiel 40. God is intimately connected and concerned with His people, His piercing gaze always on them, He searches hearts and minds.

'For the eyes of the LORD range throughout the earth to strengthen those whose hearts are fully committed to him'.
(2 Chron 16v 9)

In these future times of persecution and sacrifice, nominal Christians represented by the courts of the Gentiles have long since disappeared back into the world. They do not want to wear the sackcloth of suffering and sacrifice, preferring comfort and temporary 'security'. They have vanished without a trace, but those deeper in the worship and service of God are in the temple and especially the altar (of worship, sacrifice and representing the cross). Out of his remnant God is raising up an end time army, comprised of strong and seasoned warriors.

The two witnesses

There are many different theories about who or what the two witnesses represent. There is the obvious reference to Moses and Elijah in the signs and wonders they can perform, the ability to stop the rain for long periods of time (three and a half years? – 1 Kings 17) or send plagues (even turning water into blood – Ex 7-13). Both Moses and Elijah are giants of the prophetic world, and were transfigured with Christ (Mark 9v 2-8). They are awesome in power, not to be trifled with. We remember Paul's forceful judgements in the book of Acts. Elymas the sorcerer is blinded by Paul's word for a season (Acts 13v 11), Paul rebukes the high priest (although he quickly retracts this) 'God will strike you, you white-washed wall' (Acts 23v 3). Peter has fiery moments, lambasting Simon the sorcerer, *"May your money perish with you, because you thought you could buy the gift of God with money!* (Acts 8v 20)

The western Church is uncomfortable with judgement, but we are God's children, 'whoever touches you touches the apple of his eye' (Zech 2v 8). As the day of judgement draws near, God will overturn those who seek to interfere with His witnesses. The message is too important. Are we too concerned that nobody's feelings will be hurt? 'Niceness' is not a fruit of the spirit, there is no 'PC' culture in heaven! We will only become more unpopular as 'gross darkness covers the earth.' (Isa 60v 2). Jesus makes this abundantly clear in his teachings. Now is the time to decide if we are fully in or fully out; the Kingdom of God is no place for the lukewarm (Rev 3v 16)!

At the start of Revelation Jesus is walking among the seven lampstands which represent the seven churches. Could it be that by chapter eleven there are only two left, because of the fierce persecution that the churches have endured? God always leaves Himself a remnant. The graphic image of these churches wearing sackcloth denotes immense suffering even as they minister boldly. They also grieve for the friends and brothers they have lost, and those they know will soon be taken. There is great cost to their message. They know they could lose their lives at any moment. They also groan for the lost who stubbornly shake their fists at God. They are also likened to two olive trees, a beautiful prophetic picture echoing Zechariah (here representing Joshua and Zerubbabel).

"I see a solid gold lampstand with a bowl at the top and seven lamps on it, with seven channels to the lamps. Also there are two olive trees by it, one on the right of the bowl and the other on its left." (Zechariah 4v 2-3)

The name, witnesses, draws our attention to their impending martyrdom. The word 'martyr' in Greek means 'witness' in English, and it is used over two hundred times in the New Testament. In contemporary Church life we have watered down the meaning of 'witness' to someone who shares their faith occasionally. There is also the Old Testament legal requirement for matters of law to be decided by the witness of two or three (Deuteronomy 17v 6), an idea developed in the New Testament (Matt 18v 16, 2 Corinthians 13v 1).

Some interpretations of the two witnesses are,

- **The Church and Israel**
- **Jesus and His Church**
- **the Church and it's leadership**
- **God and His Word**
- **God and His Spirit**
- **The prophets and apostles**
- **John Wesley and George Whitfield**
- **Enoch and Elijah**

I do not have a definitive answer but I want to emphasize the prophesying and testifying that these two witnesses do. Whichever of these scenarios is right, maybe all or none, great importance is given to their mission and message. We assume they are prophesying about Jesus and His soon return, and testifying to His death, burial and resurrection. This is prophetic evangelism. They assert the truth of His Word and His Resurrection and look forward, prophetically, to the return of their conquering King.

This is their last chance to evangelise the world, and for people to respond to their message of forgiveness and hope. Fearlessly the witnesses keep proclaiming their message despite the hatred and rage it is stirring up. Prophetic evangelism is not always popular and we will not always be thanked – instead we may taste persecution. There are times we are surprised at the hostile response to the Gospel, yet we are 'an aroma that brings death' (2 Corinthians 2v 16).

The Word of God is a fire coming out of our mouths. It brings scorching conviction of sin and warning of judgement (John 16v 8).There was a point of no return for Pharaoh (we are reminded in this passage of Egypt and Sodom) when God gave him over to his own stubborn will (Ex 9v 12). It will be the same for the world before the end, there is a cut-off point, we must be sober and alert.

'Let the one who does wrong continue to do wrong; let the vile person continue to be vile; let the one who does right continue to do right; and let the holy person continue to be holy." (Rev 22v 11)

The outrage against the witnesses' message reaches a peak. The beast (satan, or one of his high ranking lieutenants) comes out of the abyss with murderous intent. Just as the beast attacked and killed Jesus he will do the same to the witnesses (John 15v 20). Is now the time to call for volunteers, this is not seeker sensitive Christianity? The witnesses were willing to pay the ultimate price of their lives (Matt 16v 25).

We will be presented with many opportunities to give up evangelising, prophesying and/or both. If we don't recognise that it is the beast (satan) attacking us through people, we will become angry and discouraged, and stop prematurely. Our battle is not against flesh and blood (Eph 6v 12). I have met so many Christians who have pulled back in bitterness and are not living in all that God called them to. I'm inspired by Stephen the deacon, who was stoned to death as he preached the gospel (Acts 6-7). There are times we must be like Jeremiah, 'I will make you a wall to this people, a fortified wall of bronze; they will fight against you but will not overcome you, for I am with you to rescue and save you," declares the LORD'. (Jer 15v 20)

The witnesses followed in the footsteps of Christ to His Cross. And like Christ (does the three and a half days speak of His three and a half year ministry?) are resurrected and taken up to God. What do we take from this? Our prophetic evangelism may grow in power and signs and wonders may accompany it; this does not mean we will be popular or that the church will grow (faster than persecution reduces it). But, like the two witnesses we must continue with courage and faithfulness until we can't any more. Evangelism and prophecy are ministries emphasized in the endtime harvest, there's no stopping, we will rest when we get to heaven. They are vital gifts and ministries to fulfil the great commission.

'And this gospel of the kingdom will be preached in the whole world as a testimony to all nations, and then the end will come'. (Matt 24v 14)

There will be times people gladly receive our message and drink it in deeply. On other occasions we will meet with persecution. What is our response?

'But you, keep your head in all situations, endure hardship, do the work of an evangelist, discharge all the duties of your ministry'. (2 Tim 4v 5)

18 Ten reasons why prophetic evangelism is for now

1. Prophetic evangelism demonstrates a personal God

Human beings have a deep (God given) need and desire to know and be known (Gen 2v 18). When God deals with us in a personal way and shows intimate knowledge of our struggles, sorrows and joys it is powerful. We're no longer talking to people about the 'concept' of God but a God Who is near, very near. In these days, generally speaking, people are less concerned about our theology (which we should still guard carefully (1 Timothy 4v 16) than with an experience with our personal, and personally-knowable, God.

'the word is very near you; it is in your mouth and in your heart so you may obey it'. (Deut 30v 14)

This anecdote is not directly prophetic evangelism but it demonstrates this principle beautifully: I was on a week's mission to Nepal and was tired towards the end of the week. I was asked to preach in a Kathmandu Church on the Sunday. God kept bringing me back to a message I had preached six months before concerning John Mark when he left Paul and Barnabas and the apostolic mission in Acts 13. I don't usually preach the same message twice, I prefer to be fresh. However, God kept prodding me about that message. Finally, on the Sunday morning I submitted to that leading and refreshed myself in that sermon as best as I could remember. The major thrust was the overcoming of fear; something in which I have authenticity and authority due to my personal testimony.

'My ears had heard of you but now my eyes have seen you' (Job 42v 5)

At the church the worship leader was somehow drawn to my attention. She was aggravating me, I can't quite say how but there was something 'off' about her and I struggled to enter into worship. I've never been 'aggravated' like this before. I was mindful of Paul and the girl with the spirit of divination in Philippi. Afterwards I preached and found freedom in my message, drawing in aspects of my own testimony. The worship leader listened spellbound with a white face.

At the end when I offered prayer she staggered forward shaking visibly. She explained her situation and I was astonished at how my testimony and her experience were intertwined. It was uncanny. As she explained, the fear gripped her even tighter and she groaned and fell writhing on the floor. I am no expert in deliverance but together with the pastor we rebuked a spirit of fear and kept going until she was revived. If I had ignored the prompting of the Holy Spirit regarding my message, maybe she would never have got this spiritual help. Her fear fixated on her imminent move to the UK, and she may never have made that trip without this release.

'The right word at the right time is like precious gold set in silver'.
(Prov 25v 11 CEV version)

2. Prophetic evangelism brings absolutes into a subjective world

"How long will you waver between two opinions? If the LORD is God, follow Him. (1 Kings 18v 21) Our postmodern world encourages a false subjectivity with 'space' for everybody's 'truth' and feelings to be accommodated. It's a delusional state, how can truth exist for one person and not another? The result of this is 'everyone does what seems right in his own eyes' (Judges 21v 25), and we have slipped very far away from God. Prophetic evangelism shatters this delusion and confronts people with objective truth. God can only know you and know things about you if He is real. He can't only be real to me! We can then answer Pilate's postmodern question 'what is truth?' The answer is not a proposition or a concept. The answer is the man, Jesus. He is the way and the truth and the life (John 14v 6).

3. Prophetic evangelism can pivot to any number of different gifts

'The wind blows wherever it pleases. You hear its sound, but you cannot tell where it comes from or where it is going. So it is with everyone born of the Spirit." (John 3v 8) We have said before how the prophetic can trigger other spiritual gifts. A word of knowledge can release faith for healing. Discerning of spirits can offer the opportunity for deliverance and pave the way for someone to be filled with the Holy Spirit. The different gifts complement and develop each other.

The prophetic connects people straight to God and His desire to heal and restore them, before their hang-ups with

Christians are triggered. By this time their guard might have come down slightly. It's sad to say that many people in our communities have been damaged in church, sometimes irreparably, unless God gets involved to heal. We can operate in the gifts without broadcasting it or mentioning that we are Christian. Discretion may be the better part of valour. These people will have an antagonistic reaction to 'Christians' and any mention of 'church'. Let's give the benefit of the doubt and remember this if we meet with hostility from someone, their history may contain bad experiences with 'Christians.' Hurting people hurt people. We don't need to take rejection personally, we probably have done nothing wrong.

4. Prophetic evangelism offers the supernatural to a generation hungry for it

We are informed by the media that the teaching of evolution has done its work and no one believes in medieval nonsense about God and angels, or the devil and hell anymore. Well, the spiritual side of humanity has not been satisfied with this, *'He has also set eternity in the human heart; yet no one can fathom what God has done from beginning to end'.* (Eccles 3v 11b)

Our society's all-consuming hunger for the occult and supernatural in film, music, arts and media is evidence of this. There are innumerable means to access spiritual information. Witchcraft is today 'mainstream'. People are streaming to new age and occult 'guides'. Our God-given spiritual hunger cannot be shut down by an ideology that denies it.

Prophetic evangelism offers a taste of a spiritual Kingdom that not only piques this hunger (as does the occult) but satisfies it with good things. There is no need for people to sacrifice their 'spirituality' in becoming Christian, it can be redeemed and become an instrument of blessing in the Kingdom of God. Christians should be the most obviously spiritual of all people, and if we're not we need to repent of this.

There's a saying we've all heard, 'he's so heavenly minded he's of no earthly use.' The exact opposite is true. Unless we can represent our spiritual kingdom on earth and demonstrate true spiritual wisdom how will anyone know who to follow. Unless we're heavenly minded Christians, we're of no earthly use! The world is looking for spirituality, let's give them the real thing.

5. Prophetic evangelism can operate in almost every situation

Every circumstance is an opportunity for this method of evangelism. It's *'to proclaim Your loving devotion in the morning, and Your faithfulness at night',* (Psalm 92v 2)

a case of leaning into God, seeing what He is doing and joining in, catching the 'wave' of His activity. Other methods of evangelism can be more formulaic, which is helpful, we can fall back on that. If we're flowing with God we can be amazed where we end up, weaving in and out with different methods as He shows us. Prophetic evangelism is fluid, working alongside all styles, the gospel message is supreme.

When I say it can work in all situations, I should qualify this, if we are at a secular workplace, working for our boss needs to be our priority. We are not being paid to function as a prophetic evangelist, and if we act like we are; doing the 'right' thing is the wrong thing. Our work ethic and commitment to team is our 'gospel'. However, if we are exemplary employees, we may well find we're given opportunities to explain why that is the case, which leads us into our prophetic evangelism. Even if the world does not recognise or love our God, they will appreciate our Godly values expressed in the workplace!

Sometimes we can feel that we've failed if we don't mention Jesus, God, Christianity or Church in a conversation. On one train journey I sat opposite an elderly man whose jacket was covered with sewed on CND, socialist, and communist badges; a student's coat! We got into a lovely conversation, he was a kind man who cared deeply about the poor. Ten minutes in I thought that I really should mention that I am a Christian.

So I found a way to introduce it into the conversation. The impact was instant and profound. He stopped talking to me immediately, mid-sentence, broke off eye contact, stopped smiling and his body language shouted he wanted nothing more to do with me.

At the time I felt hurt, how could he suddenly stonewall me like that? The change was dramatic. But in hindsight I realised my internal pressure to make the conversation overtly 'Christian' was the problem. He clearly had a spiritual block and sensitivity was required. We can be our own worst enemies! I wished I had asked God what he wanted me to do, rather than assuming I knew.

6. Prophetic evangelism can be used 'under the radar'

"I am sending you out like sheep among wolves. Therefore be as shrewd as snakes and as innocent as doves.' (Matt 10v 16)

I knew an Argentinian Christian who would offer prayer on the London Underground. Instead of introducing himself as a Christian he would strike up a conversation and say that he had spiritual power. He would then offer to lay hands on people for their physical or psychological issues. He was not someone who would be easily deflected and many people accepted his prayer. Only then would he use the name of Jesus, and follow up with overt evangelism. Is this deceptive or an ingenious way to bypass people's presuppositions about Christians?

I suppose the answer to that depends on whether he was Spirit led, which he was. He got to pray for a lot of people who might have refused if he had been conspicuously Christian at first.

7. Prophetic evangelism requires us to walk closely with Jesus

We all want to walk closely with Jesus. There are days when we find it a joy and delight to do so, there's no effort involved. Sometimes though God seems far away, we are busy in our work and don't feel that intimate connection.

"Draw me after you and let us run together!' (Song of Songs 1v 4)

Prophetic evangelism's emphasis on listening to God and not relying on any preconceived formula cannot function for long if we're not close to His heart. It's an oxymoron. We're only as good on any given day as we are hearing and seeing Jesus.

If we spend time with God in our private place, He will walk with us in the public place. There are no shortcuts, we can't short-circuit getting to know God and discerning His voice. I have a friend who is a man of prayer in his seventies. He has pastored the same church for forty years and gets up early every morning to spend time with God. He is noted for his intercessory ministry. I was struck when he said to me, with all seriousness; 'I wouldn't say that I know God'. God help us in our days of sound bites, tweets and drive-through everything. The most precious thing we have to offer to Jesus is our time.

Prophetic evangelism is a lifestyle, it grows as we practice alongside spending quality and quantity time with God. It only functions out of revelation and we can embrace the fact that it forces us back to God at times when we might otherwise disengage by default. Regular unhurried communication is essential for any healthy relationship. Our evangelism is the overflow of this, we must prioritise His presence.

8. Prophetic evangelism grabs people's attention

Recent research suggests that today the average person has an attention span of less than seven seconds. What are we doing to ourselves with all our technology? In any case, we don't have long to engage with someone and if they

'They were amazed at his teaching, because his words had authority'. (Luke 4v 32)

disengage with us we may never get them back again. A word of knowledge or prophecy can break into someone's private bubble long enough for us to hold their attention and share the gospel with them, otherwise we're potentially just mouthing words.

Imagine if we could walk up to a complete stranger and say, 'your name is Norman Wright, you work in scientific research and have a crumbling hip.' Assuming we are right, we have grabbed that man by the proverbial jugular. Might he be willing to listen to me now? The famous healing evangelist of the 1900's, William Branham, moved in this level of revelation, he could give strangers incredible details about their lives. This was not an end in itself, but a bridge to drive the gospel over.

You might say, that's a massive risk, I'll never operate like that. Maybe, maybe not. But if we're not aiming for something we won't move in the right direction. My experience is that as we are faithful and bold in the use of a gift, God graciously adds to it. We must start from where we are!

9. Prophetic evangelism is exciting and faith building for us

'The seventy-two returned with joy'
(Luke 10v 17a)

Terrifying, life affirming, bottom clenching, the times when I have stepped out in prophetic evangelism have left me wondering why I don't do it more.

The plane was idling on the tarmac, we were flying back from Crete to England. The plane was full and everyone in a good mood after their holiday. Bec and I were seated next to a young woman who was lamenting to her friends in front of us about a skin issue she had on her hand, the Cretan sun hadn't cleared it up. Before I had even finished my thought my heart starting racing. I knew I had to offer to pray for her. Saying that I was a Christian and that God can heal skin issues I prayed quietly but definitely in the name of Jesus for her healing. Then the silence was awful. For the next four hours I squirmed in the seat next to her, praying God please touch her hand. I stole a look at it every now and again, I could still see the boils. I was silently pulling on God in prayer, 'Lord this girl and her friends heard me pray in Jesus name, please do something, show her how much you love her'.

With relief I disembarked but at every turn we bumped into her and her friends again. Even at baggage reclaim I couldn't avoid her as I wished. That hand had hours of prayer and I believe God will do something. I refused to believe nothing happened. What, I may never know.

The beautiful simplicity of trusting that my Father is speaking to me and I can step out onto the water *is where I want to live from.* I find Jesus is there, already waiting, to back up my fumbling efforts and remind me how good He is. My faith has been 'earthed' into the reality of daily life, it's authentic and real! *The insidious pressure to have a 'theoretical' Christianity which is 'technical atheism' is broken once again.* The best time to hear God is when we've just obeyed Him. Delayed obedience yields limited fruit and tends to 'wax' up the ears.

'He who did not spare His own Son but gave Him up for us all, how will He not also, along with Him, freely give us all things?' (Romans 8v 32)

10. Prophetic evangelism glorifies Christ

I am happy to have been on the receiving end of prophetic evangelism. During our year in South London I spent one day a week in Chislehurst serving a church in evangelism. Ordinarily I drove the eight miles by car which took thirty

'You will always harvest what you plant' (Gal 6v 7b)

minutes, but one week Bec needed the car. In South London it isn't always straightforward on public transport to go east to west or vice versa. I needed to go up to London Bridge and then down to Chislehurst, a journey of one hour and fifty minutes. I was sitting on the platform at London Bridge inwardly bemoaning this fact when a stranger came alongside me and crouched down to my level. 'God wants to speak to you' he said naturally. 'Great, I replied, I'm a Christian', wanting to assert which 'God' I listen to. 'Yes, so am I' he continued. 'There's a change coming for your ministry, and it's going to be big. God is drawing close to you and wants you to hear His heart.'

I thanked him profusely and off he went. This message made the ludicrously long journey more than worthwhile; God had a prophetic appointment for me at London Bridge. Although at the time I couldn't see where this 'word' might fit, I was suitably encouraged and shelved the word in my mental folder named 'This may make sense later'. In hindsight I can see it was a preparatory word prophesying my new job as full time evangelist which commenced seven months later. On that chilly morning at London Bridge I didn't know this job even existed.

I flatter myself that this change ultimately brings glory to God. More people are going to hear the gospel. My family and I being in the right place, at the right time, and with me in the right vocation, equates to fruitfulness in the Kingdom of God. A big change often involves implicit risk and sacrifice which God more than rewards us for if we are willing to make it. For a prophetic evangelist, souls are the great prize and reward.

The ultimate purpose of all prophetic evangelism is to reveal the glory of God in Christ. (2 Cor 4v 6)

19 *Revealing Jesus*

In the year that King Uzziah died, I saw the Lord, high and exalted, seated on a throne; and the train of his robe filled the temple. Above him were seraphim, each with six wings: With two wings they covered their faces, with two they covered their feet, and with two they were flying. And they were calling to one another:

"Holy, holy, holy is the Lord Almighty; the whole earth is full of his glory." (Isaiah 6v1-3)

In this final chapter we will encourage ourselves in the Person and perfection of Christ. All our ministry flows from the delight of knowing Him and making Him known. What is the goal of our prophetic evangelism? Our purpose can be summed up in the desire to glorify Jesus and make Him gloriously known to humanity (Eph 1v 10). Jesus not only has the answers to the world's ills and the deep brokenness of mankind. He is the answer, Himself.

What is it specifically we need to reveal through our lives and ministry about Jesus? What do we need to be mindful of as we step out in prophetic evangelism?

His radiance

Jesus' glory is radiated out into the world through His people. We are His glorious bride on the earth, full of His Spirit and washed in His Word, shining out His presence. Just as Moses face shone as he came down from the mountain (Ex 34v 35), so ours shine as we spend time in God's presence. We can only tell people as much as we know; we can only lead them as far as we have gone, so the better we know Jesus the more effectively we'll make His glory known. The great commandment (Matt 22v 37) comes before the great commission (Mark 16v 15-16).

'The Son is the image of the invisible God, the firstborn over all creation'. (Col 1v 15)

The glory of God is the manifestation of His goodness. Moses requested to see the glory of God and God let all His goodness pass before

'My ears had heard of you but now my eyes have seen you'. (Job 42 v5) him (Ex 33v 19). As we taste and see that the Lord is good (Psalm 34v 8), we can introduce Jesus with authenticity, 'this is my lover and this is my friend' (Song of Songs 5v 16). The prophetic reveals God's goodness, evangelism tells of His goodness; His arms are outstretched beckoning all to come to Him (Romans 10v 21).

Let us come fully into the light of His presence and allow Him to deal with anything in us that could cloud His glory. Jesus said to Philip, 'Anyone who has seen me has seen the Father' (John 14v 9). Would that we could say the same thing! Through our countenance, our conduct and our communication we can mirror Jesus out into the world. The world needs to see Jesus lifted up (John 12v 32) and where else can they look for Him, but in the church of Christ? We are His body here on the earth (Romans 12v 4-5). I could count on both hands the times when people have said to me, in as many words, your face is glowing (with God). How often is it concern, confusion and disbelief they see there? I want this to change, so that I can say 'imitate me, just as I imitate Christ' (1 Cor 11v 1).

The Son is the radiance of God's glory and the exact representation of His being, sustaining all things by His powerful word. After He had provided purification for sins, He sat down at the right hand of the Majesty in heaven'.
(Hebrews 1v 3)

His righteousness

"There is no one righteous, not even one;
there is no one who understands;
there is no one who seeks God.
All have turned away,
they have together become worthless;
there is no one who does good, not even one."
(Romans 3v 10–12)

There is only One who is right with God, only One standing in perfection before His Father and that is Christ Jesus. Only clothed in His righteousness can we stand, not through any merit of ours. He alone can make us right with God, only He has the answers for our lost world. Human kindness and mercy will not 'cut it' (Isaiah 64v 6). Our disease is much deadlier and uglier than that, there are no fig leaves that can cover it (Genesis 3v 7). 'Without the shedding of blood there is no remission of sins' (Hebrews 9v 22).

'And the righteousness of God is through faith from Jesus Christ toward

all those believing. For there is no distinction. For all have sinned and fallen short of the glory of God.' (Romans 3v 22–23)

First, we have Jesus' righteousness imputed to us. He deals with our unrighteousness, separating us from it,

"Come now, let us settle the matter," says the LORD. "Though your sins are like scarlet, they shall be as white as snow; though they are red as crimson, they shall be like wool'. (Isa 1v 18)

Then He imparts; He fills and clothes us in His righteousness,

'God made Him who had no sin to be sin for us, so that in Him we might become the righteousness of God'. (2 Cor 5v 21)

Repentance

Only deep repentance leads to discipleship. Shallow conversions breed weak and even unbelieving believers. Where there is not the reality of sin being dealt with, Christians don't mature and grow. We repent until we start to bear the fruit of repentance. The gospel we preach and our prophecy must include the call for repentance; we keep repenting until we bear fruit in accordance with repentance (Matthew 3v 8). Our prophetic evangelism will bring the lost into the valley of decision (Joel 3v 14). It's no longer an issue of whether God is real or not, but are they willing to follow Him, or not? The fear of God falls on people as they realise they are known (Prov 9v 10). Prophetic evangelism brings God very close to them.

'Or do you show contempt for the riches of his kindness, forbearance and patience, not realizing that God's kindness is intended to lead you to repentance?' (Romans 2 v 4).

The offer of salvation is open to all. There is no-one beyond the reach of God's grace, the blood of Jesus can cleanse the worst sinner who sincerely repents. We do not know who will repent, we leave that to our omniscient God. Let's generously preach the Gospel of Salvation refusing to be discouraged by rejection or threats. Then once we've done our part let's trust God to do His part.

'for, "Everyone who calls on the name of the Lord will be saved." (Rom 10v 13)

His resurrection

' If there is no resurrection of the dead, then not even Christ has been raised. And if Christ has not been raised, our preaching is useless and so is your faith. More than that, we are then found to be false witnesses about God, for we have testified about God that he raised Christ from the dead. (1 Cor 15v 13–15)

Prophetic evangelism shouts out the message, He's alive, He's alive, He's alive. He's the same yesterday, today and forever (Heb 13v 8). The New Testament pulsates with the message of resurrection, resurrection, resurrection. Our living Christ speaks with intimate knowledge and love to His creation. He is the good news of the gospel.

The Resurrection proves the efficacy of the Cross. All God's promises are 'yes' and 'amen' because He has defeated the grave (2 Corinthians 1v 20). Jesus has crushed the serpent's head (Genesis 3v 15).

His redemption

In Christ, God reaches into the darkness of the most tangled circumstances of our pasts and brings forgiveness, healing and redemption.

'It is a fact that God has delivered us from the power of darkness – that is, Satan's kingdom – and conveyed us into the kingdom of Christ. Thus we have redemption – our sins are forgiven. We are no longer in Satan's territory, nor are we under his authority.' (D.Prince)

Jesus specializes in redemption. He takes our broken relationships, families, and churches and excavates expertly through the ruins. His work is painstaking, and slow sometimes to our way of thinking, but thorough and beautiful. It's worth the wait.

"In that day I will restore the fallen tent of David. I will repair its gaps, restore its ruins, and rebuild it as in the days of old,' (Amos 9v 11)

'But he knows the way that I take; when he has tested me, I will come forth as gold'. (Job 23v 10)

There's no financial disaster, disastrous decision, or sin committed against us that Jesus can't sift through to bring order and restoration. It's His delight to take people from the rubbish heap, cleanse them, heal them, restore them and then reveal His glory through them

With every person that Christ redeems, every area of our lives, every relationship, every pain and trial that He turns into glory, He prophesies the final and great redemption of the world. There will be a new heaven and a new earth. Christ Jesus will fully and perfectly redeem all the damage of sin and undo death and destruction. There will be no more devil or trace of darkness; pain and shame are banished forever.

'Then I saw "a new heaven and a new earth," for the first heaven and the first earth had passed away, and there was no longer any sea. I saw the Holy City, the new Jerusalem, coming down out of heaven from God, prepared as a bride beautifully dressed for her husband'. (Rev 21v 1–2)

His rest

Jesus has won the cosmic war. At the cross He cried 'It is finished'. When

He ascended to the Father He was seated at His right hand side, the place of honour. He did this because His mission was successfully completed, He has eternally broken the back of death, hell, sin and the grave. Jesus has bought with His own blood the right for you and me to be called sons of God. We are welcomed back into relationship with the Father when we choose Jesus, because Jesus is the Chosen One and we are in Him (1 Peter 2v 4). We must extend this invitation to all.

'Exalted to the right hand of God, he has received from the Father the promised Holy Spirit and has poured out what you now see and hear'.
(Acts 2v 33)

Our spiritual warfare commences from the vantage point of the victory of Calvary and our resurrected Christ. 'Judah's lion has burst his chains' ('Ye choirs of New Jerusalem', St. Fulbert of Chartres). The war is won. We are seated with Him in heavenly places (Eph 2v 6). Now we have a few skirmishes and battles with defeated foes. They rage and panic in their death throes (Rev 12v 12) while we fight for the lost who don't know their right hand from their left (Jonah 4v 11).

Some battles we win, some we lose and some we're not entirely sure what's happened. But we fight entirely certain of ultimate victory in the war. Christ is the captain of our salvation and He has overcome in every way, bursting out of the tomb so that we can follow Him into eternity. In this reality we find our rest. Because Jesus is at rest, so are we, our 'rest' is active and powerful (Heb 4v 11).

'Where, O death, is your victory? Where, O death, is your sting?"
(1 Cor 15v 55)

His soon return

It's supremely appropriate to conclude this book with a prophetic reminder and evangelistic encouragement that soon Jesus will return. For the joy set before us we can easily endure the momentary trials we experience (Heb 12v 2). The end of the book (the Bible) is but the beginning of an eternity with Him. We're going to live forever with Him in a beautiful world made new. There will be no more crying, sighing or dying or pain; only unbroken fellowship with Jesus (Rev 21).

Let's tell as many people as we can, in as many ways as we can, with as much passion and skill as we can and in as many places as we can. It's time to get right with Jesus. It is the highest call and greatest privilege to tell people about our King. Time is short. Without any new prophecy we can safely say we're closer today to His return than we have ever been. Let's get right with Him and exhort others to do the same. Jesus stands at the crossroads holding out His hands (Jeremiah 6v 16). Let's not allow any to miss the day of our visitation (Luke 19v 44). Today is the day of Salvation (2 Corinthians 6v 2). Come Lord Jesus!

'Then the angel showed me the river of the water of life, as clear as crystal, flowing from the throne of God and of the Lamb down the middle of the great street of the city. On each side of the river stood the tree of life, bearing twelve crops of fruit, yielding its fruit every month. And the leaves of the tree are for the healing of the nations. No longer will there be any curse. The throne of God and of the Lamb will be in the city, and his servants will serve him. They will see his face, and his name will be on their foreheads. There will be no more night. They will not need the light of a lamp or the light of the sun, for the Lord God will give them light. And they will reign for ever and ever...

"I, Jesus, have sent my angel to give you this testimony for the churches. I am the Root and the Offspring of David, and the bright Morning Star." The Spirit and the bride say, "Come!" And let the one who hears say, "Come!" Let the one who is thirsty come; and let the one who wishes take the free gift of the water of life. I warn everyone who hears the words of the prophecy of this scroll: If anyone adds anything to them, God will add to that person the plagues described in this scroll. And if anyone takes words away from this scroll of prophecy, God will take away from that person any share in the tree of life and in the Holy City, which are described in this scroll. He who testifies to these things says, "Yes, I am coming soon." Amen. Come, Lord Jesus. The grace of the Lord Jesus be with God's people. Amen'. (Rev 22 v1-6, 16-21)

Appendices

appendix 1

Definition of
Prophetic Evangelism

Prophetic Evangelism is a term not found in Scripture. Nor is the term "the trinity", "the rapture", "Easter", "common grace", "holy communion", "replacement theology", "Christmas". We could go on. There are many terms and doctrines developed by the broad church that assist in the outworking of daily Christian life and praxis in this world where we must live and witness. Prophetic Evangelism is one of these, we suggest.

It is helpful to define our term for clarity, so people know what it is, and what it is not.

Prophetic Evangelism is an approach to sharing the good news of Jesus (evangelism) using specifically those prophetic tools and gifting provided by the Holy Spirit to the evangelist.

It is an approach to evangelism that seeks to meet the needs and/or circumstances of an individual who does not yet know Jesus as Lord and as Saviour by touching their life or circumstances with knowledge, insights and counseling that is by its nature supernatural (n.b. of the Holy Spirit) rather than through human wisdom, experience or insight. (Prophetic Evangelism may by God's grace and pleasure be used in conjunction with "natural" human wisdom, but will elevate or magnify such "natural" wisdom to meet the actual need or circumstance of the non-Christian to whom the prophetic insight is addressed).

Prophetic tools are also a blessing in counseling and ministry to other Christians, but Prophetic *Evangelism* is specifically a Spirit-given tool to bless the non-Christian (non-believer). The message delivered through Prophetic Evangelism is (almost always) God's way of directly challenging an individual and lead them to recognize a definitive decision point in their life.

Whilst many (most?) re-births (John 3: 3 and 7) are the result of a process that has taken years, and through ongoing relationship with a believer(s) to reach fruition, Prophetic Evangelism can sometimes lead to a very dramatic immediate decision for Christ.

Gifts of the Spirit are provided to enable and magnify our ability to serve in this world. Message of wisdom, message of knowledge, faith, gifts of healing, miraculous powers, prophecy, distinguishing between spirits, different kinds of tongues, interpretations of tongues, administration (1 Cor 12: 4-11 and 28; Romans 12: 6-8). All gifts overlap and are evidenced in greater or lesser degree in the lives of all believers.

Prophetic Evangelism is a compound gift touching particularly on *message of wisdom, *message of knowledge, *prophecy, * distinguishing between spirits.

appendix 2

**Prophetic Evangelism
– Gifts**

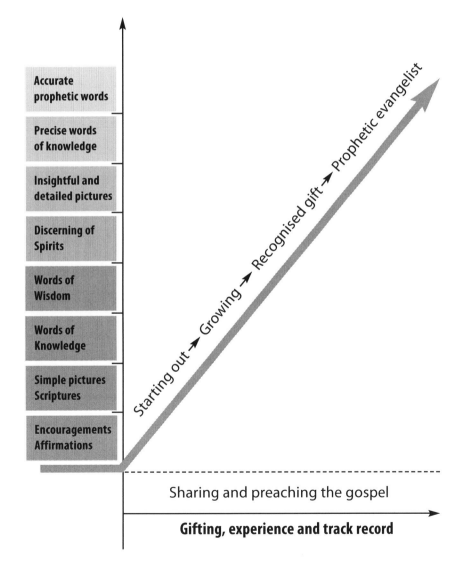

Accurate prophetic words

Precise words of knowledge

Insightful and detailed pictures

Discerning of Spirits

Words of Wisdom

Words of Knowledge

Simple pictures Scriptures

Encouragements Affirmations

Starting out → Growing → Recognised gift → Prophetic evangelist

Sharing and preaching the gospel

Gifting, experience and track record

appendix 3

**Examples of
Prophetic Evangelism**

Type	Description	Example
Accurate prophetic words	Revelation of the future which is both accurate and faith building.	'In six months time you will put your house up for sale, you intend to move to Canada to work in banking. Someone will make an immediate offer on your house, do not accept it, they are not trustworthy. Wait for the next offer which will be lower but genuine'.
Precise words of knowledge	Accurate information about the past or the present. A level of detail that proves, beyond all doubt, that God is speaking.	'You have a set of keys in your pocket. One of the keys is linked to a property that you are renting out. You are having stressful discussions with your tenants, their surname is Taylor. In fact, they have threatened to sue you and you don't know what to do. You are breathless when you see unexpected letters on your doormat'.
Insightful and detailed pictures	Pictures which profoundly speak into the deeper emotions, struggles and joys of the person are concerned.	'There is a staircase you are thinking of climbing but there is a strong fear associated with it and you tempted to hide in the cupboard under the stairs'.

continued on next page

Type	Description	Example
Discerning of spirits	A spritual sense/awareness of something that is spiritually or emotionally present. Sometimes this is positive, perhaps sensing a strength in the person, but other times negative. Discern redemptive giftings and callings.	Sensing that someone has a crushed spirit, related to bereavement. Or a rebellious spirit. We don't necessarily need to directly challenge it but it helps us navigate the conversation skilfully. We might need to bind it up through prayer in our mind. Discerning spirits will make sense of contradictions in the person's conversation. Someone has a gift of worship, 'You are very creative and artistic and you feel freed up in music. God wants to lead you in this'. (The person becomes animated and engaged).
Words of wisdom	Like a hot knife slicing through butter a word of wisdom can bring clarity, perspective and a solution to a knotty problem.	'If you can find a way to forgive what has been done to you, your body will come into rest. Your blood pressure will come down and your allergies will recede until they finally disappear'
Words of knowledge	Revelation about events past or present in a person's life and family	'You've lost people you love and it has made you frightened in relationships', 'Your job security has been very uncertain, and you've been losing sleep. God is going to move you to a place where your skills can shine out'.

continued on next page

Type	Description	Example
Simple pictures, scriptures.	A simple spiritual picture which speaks to the wants, needs, concerns and struggles of the person/people.	'You are a caterpillar in a chrysalis struggling and despairing of ever getting out but you will be a beautiful butterfly emerging and flying high. You are at a crossroads in your life and questioning what to do. God wants to take your hand and show you the. right way. A scripture indicative of God's love and concern (e.g. from Psalm 139). 'You are not an accident, God formed you in your mother's womb and has a great purpose for your life'.
Encouragements, affirmations	Spritual encouragements. In a fatherless generation with many spiritual orphans, affirmation is particularly powerful.	'You have a gift of befriending people. You are a creative person. You are kind. It was amazing you forgave that.'
	SHARING AND PREACHING THE GOSPEL	Taking every opportunity through our whole lives to model/share/exemplify, and speak out the gospel.

appendix4

**Prophetic Evangelism
– Growth**

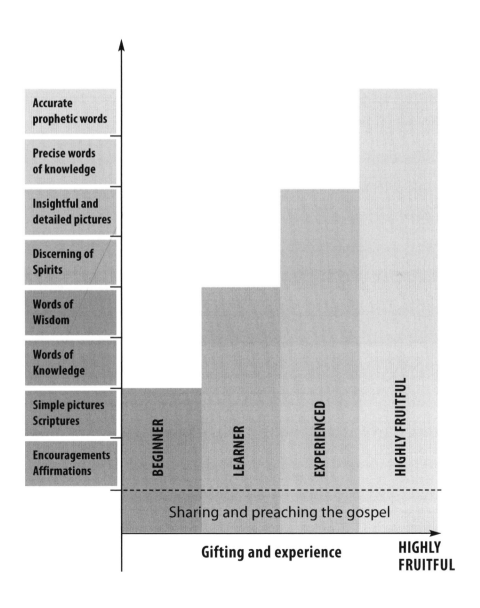

Accurate prophetic words

Precise words of knowledge

Insightful and detailed pictures

Discerning of Spirits

Words of Wisdom

Words of Knowledge

Simple pictures Scriptures

Encouragements Affirmations

BEGINNER

LEARNER

EXPERIENCED

HIGHLY FRUITFUL

Sharing and preaching the gospel

Gifting and experience

HIGHLY FRUITFUL

appendix 5

Prophecy – Continuum

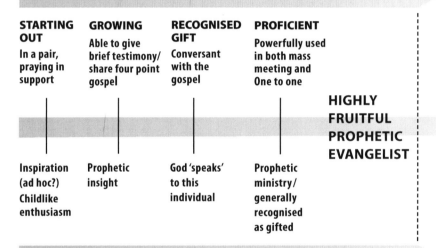

Deepening exposure to God's Word

STARTING OUT	GROWING	RECOGNISED GIFT	PROFICIENT
In a pair, praying in support	Able to give brief testimony/ share four point gospel	Conversant with the gospel	Powerfully used in both mass meeting and One to one

HIGHLY FRUITFUL PROPHETIC EVANGELIST

Inspiration (ad hoc?) Childlike enthusiasm	Prophetic insight	God 'speaks' to this individual	Prophetic ministry/ generally recognised as gifted

Deepening intimacy with God's Holy Spirit

Prophecy is not one dimensional. As suggested here, it can range from the ad-hoc or provisional , where God graciously provides a degree of understanding, perhaps unexpectedly "out of the blue", through to a very clear and pronounced anointing where an individual has a prominent prophetic gift. But there is also a dotted line, beyond which the modern 'prophet' cannot develop. Modern prophecy is not a revelation from God in the sense of Scripture which must of necessity have an eternal dimension, speaking of God's over-arching salvation plan and purposes.

Note that several criteria are set out in Scripture to characterize the true from the false prophetic e.g. (1) prophecy must be in continuity with the customs and traditions of Israel as enshrined in the Torah – Deut 13: 1-5; 18:20; Isaiah 8: 20; Romans 12: 6) (2) the prophet must speak only that which God commands (Deut 18:20) and (3) true prophecy must be historically verified (Deut 18:21-22; Jer 28:8-9).

For these reasons, the words of a modern prophet, no matter how profound they may be, are not considered canon as are the words expressed in Scripture, and which must be pronounced as closed (Revelation 22: 18-19).

We note that deepening experience of, and application of, the prophetic will always be a "product" of deepening exposure to God's Word and deepening exposure to God's Spirit. If expressed in mathematical terms it is as though it is Word x Spirit = Prophecy.

In this diagram above, we suggest some descriptions of what this might mean to Jesus' modern followers .....

appendix 6

Prophecy – one coin, two sides...

Gifting to interpret with precision world events and current affairs in terms of God's over-arching Salvation plan. ("where are we on God's timetable?"

Gifting to "see" into particular circumstances with God's perspective – possibly with an answer or a 'word of knowledge' for an individual or situation. ("Godly insight)"

The task of the prophet is to see and talk-out God's purposes. There is both a "macro" and "micro" dynamic in this. World events might be termed "macro". Localised situations and circumstances might be termed "micro". Either way, the prophet is seeing the situation with a clarity that the Holy Spirit provides – and then sharing this insight with the person, or people, who need to "hear." The Bible is largely concerned with the "macro"; the prophetic evangelist largely with the "micro".

appendix 7

Prophetic Journey

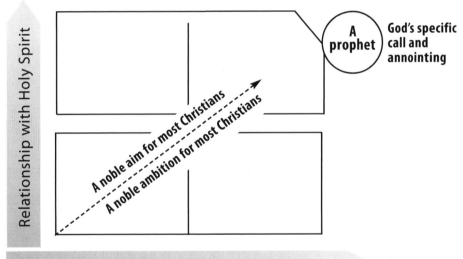

Stepping out in faith – practice makes perfect

Relationship with Holy Spirit

A prophet — God's specific call and annointing

A noble aim for most Christians

A noble ambition for most Christians

Exposure to – love of – God's word (Scripture)

Are all believers required to exercise prophetic gifts? The answer is 'no' as we see in 1 Corinthians 12: 4-11 (but note also verse 31). In the sense explored in this book Prophetic Evangelism is an amalgam of message of wisdom, message of knowledge, distinguishing between spirits and prophecy. They overlap!

Expressed mathematically we might think of it as Faith x Word x Spirit = Prophecy. It appears to be that those who determine to "grow" in grace are more likely to receive and use prophetic gifts. And some, even today, might fairly be called "prophets".

appendix 8

Biblical Prophecy and Prophetic Evangelism

Biblical prophecy

Reveals God's full purposes

Sets out the future

Nothing to be added

Prophetic Evangelism

Prophetic evangelism = a tool

= a distinct message for individual people today

Biblical prophecy stands eternally – it is a fixed canon and is recorded as such. Prophetic Evangelism by contrast links the needs and exigencies of the present with the pre-existing biblical pattern, showing characteristics of the biblical, yet applied directly to today's needs and challenges. In that sense, alone, they 'overlap' as we have sought to depict in the above.

appendix 9

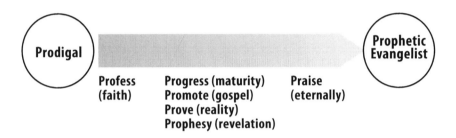

A noble ambition?

We might understand that in our Christian journey from the time we are born again ("saved") into God's eternal Kingdom, via what theologians call sanctification, we will mature and grow as we step out in faith. It is a "journey" where we move in the Spirit's flow and gain progressively in maturity. The more we mature, the greater prominence will the prophetic feature in our work and in our witness.

appendix 10

False Teaching on the Prophetic

To some extent we are all a product of the teaching we have received. Some insist 'I take it straight from the Bible'. This sounds admirable but may disguise an un-teachable spirit. We all need help in understanding what the Bible is saying through the thoroughly biblical ministry of teaching. Some of the Bible can be very hard to understand (John 6v 60, 2 Peter 3v 15-16). It is prideful to refuse help. Pride is deadly and leaves us wide open to deception (Prov 16v 18). Jesus's conversations with the Pharisees certainly bore this out (Matt 23). We all need inspired Biblical teaching to grow strong (1 Tim 5v 17b).

The teaching we receive can carry the unconscious prejudices of our leaders and so influence us either for or against prophecy. Pastors often have negative experiences in their past with excesses in this area. Local church teaching does not necessarily represent the wider church, or even the Bible, on the prophetic. We need Holy Spirit discernment. Our learning and our personal preferences must bow to the Word of God. We must refine, therefore, the silver from the dross (Psalm 12v 6), and the sacred from the vile (Jer 15v 19b).

Not many pastors would admit that they don't want the Holy Spirit and/or prophecy in their churches, even if this is exactly how they feel. A Christian friend was looking for a church in a new area and told the local vicar he wanted a 'Spirit-filled' church. The vicar firmly replied, 'well, I hope you find the church you are looking for'. Tragic, but at least he was not hypocritical. How many of our churches are technically 'open' to the Spirit when,in reality, the door is firmly closed (Rev 3v 20). If we have been in a church like this, it will probably have affected us negatively.

When I was in a season of applying for jobs (mostly pastor roles) I learnt to ask two questions immediately. One was 'do you want, or do you have the vibrant expression of the gifts of the Spirit in your church?' The answers were illuminating, and frightening! Some churches are full of beautiful Christians who have not been taught the whole truth concerning Holy Spirit and His gifts.

My purpose here is to briefly flag up the possibility that we may have imbibed false teaching somewhere along the line, so we can retrace our steps and unpick this. I believe there are four key 'vectors' directed against the gift of prophecy:

1) CESSATION TEACHING

This doctrine maintains that the gifts of the Spirit including prophecy, ended after the death of the apostles. They ceased! The miracles and healings 'launched' the church and were then withdrawn. This is a highly damaging deception based on a false exegesis of Paul's teaching on prophecy. The truth is we shall urgently need all these gifts until we stand face to face with God in eternity.

Love never fails. But where there are prophecies, they will cease; where there are tongues, they will be stilled; where there is knowledge, it will pass away...For now we only see a reflection as in a mirror, then we shall see face to face. (1 Cor 13v 8, 12).

What would a cessationalist think of people who claim to be exercising the gifts freely today? At best they are well meaning but deceived, at worst they must be operating from a source other than God.

But some of them said, "By Beelzebul, the prince of demons, he is driving out demons." (Luke 11v 15)

If we have been drinking from this theological stream, it will inevitably restrict our enjoyment and impede our freedom in these gifts. Might we need to repent for believing such teaching, even if we didn't actively seek it?

A determination not to be deceived (otherwise to be commended) can become an overweening stronghold that strangles the spiritual life out of congregations, stifling the Spirit. God will lead those who want to be led, and guide them away from false teaching. We do need humbly to challenge false teaching and, if it is not corrected, remove ourselves graciously from that church or ministry. Being personally immersed in the Word of God is our greatest protection and provision.

2) REFORM TEACHING

This teaching originates from a commendable desire to return to the Word of God, the Word only. The inherent danger is that the love of the written 'word' and Godly desire to deeply understand it can sometimes stray into idolatry, 'bibliolatry'. As much as we love and honour the Word of God, it is given to lead us into relationship with the living Word, Jesus. He still speaks today, His Spirit is alive and well. Reformed doctrine might unintentionally minimize this reality, and even militate against it.

You study the Scriptures diligently because you think that in them you have eternal life. These are the very Scriptures that testify about me, yet you refuse to come to me to have life. (John 5 39–40)

Spectrum: how Churches relate to spiritual gifts – especially prophecy.

	Extremely cautious, unlikley to receive prophecy.	Cautiously open, but unlikely to teach on the subject or encourage it.	Recognising and rejoicing in the activity of the Spirit and receiving prophecy.	Expecting there to be prophetic utterance at every gathering, some of a high level.	Lots of manifest-ations, emphasis on the Spirit.	Undiscern-ing embracing of spirituality, no longer mainstream Christianity.	
No interest/ Suspicious/ Warned off this/ Humanistic?	Needs good Biblical teaching.				Needs good Biblical teaching.		**New age/ Mysticism/ Occultic/ Immorality/ Sensuality**

Healthy fields for teaching and training

Biblical and practical framework

Deception/ False teaching	**?**	**Balance and spiritual health**	Deception/ False teaching

Before I touch on the other end of this teaching spectrum, I emphasize my love of prophecy, and passion to see it operating Biblically, especially alongside evangelism. Hopefully, this leaps off every page of this book. However, both Scripture and church history offer us many warnings that the enemy will always counterfeit the movement of God, to deceive even the elect if it were possible (Matt 24v 24). It's impossible to have 'tidy church as usual' and the superabundant activity of the Spirit (Prov 14v 14). But we must also guard vigilantly against deception (1 Tim 6v 20).

At a prophecy conference the minister gave me some Godly wisdom; 'It's extremely important that you guard whose teachings and leadership you follow. Don't accept any old thing.' These days with the acceleration of the worldwide web Christians are feeding themselves independently via all sorts of sources; good, bad and ugly (Prov 13v 20).

3) GNOSTIC TEACHING

Gnosticism or 'Knowledge' is the name given to the false teaching which immediately attacked the purity of the gospel in the fledgling church. Gnosticism purports to add 'special knowledge' and/or 'revelation' to the gospel; a gospel within the gospel, but denying it's power. This 'esoteric knowledge' is given equal if not greater weight than the revealed Word of God. It spreads through an inner circle of those who 'understand', and naturally appeals to pride. Many, if not all the epistles are counteracting this teaching in some way. John confronts gnosticism head-on, with it's total absence of morality and denial of salvation by grace through faith.

It is notable that the founders of cults are often Christians or Biblically literate people with au nformed prophetic gift (eg. Joseph Smith and Mormonism; Ellen White and the Seventh Day Adventists). If used without due reference to and reverence for the Bible, prophecy lends itself to this deception of 'special knowledge'. Extra-Biblical revelation supported by false teaching promotes another gospel, which is no gospel at all (Gal 1v 6-8). Gnosticism reinvents itself to attack and undermine the church in every stage of its development, including today (1 John 2v 22)!

4) NEW AGE SPIRITUALITY

Those who love the things of the Spirit and have experienced the power of God may not realise they bring their unsanctified spirituality into the Kingdom with them. This applies to new believers, and newly revived Christians (re:Chapter 5). Without good teaching and a thorough knowledge of Scripture any 'spiritual' experience can be embraced by well-meaning but deceived Christians. The enemy is most dangerous when he comes as an angel of light (2 Cor 11v 14). Without help they will slip anchor further and further from authentic Christianity, causing confusion and catastrophe everywhere.

One 'evangelist' who works in new age fairs and festivals insists that tarot cards amongst other occult things are not necessarily wrong; in fact he let trusted people 'read' his cards. He felt more at home with new agers and white witches than most Christians. I was flabbergasted at the level of deception! He seemed to have long since thrown out the Bible.

So, if you think you are standing firm, be careful that you don't fall! (1 Cor 10v 12)

There are also false prophets (Matt 24v 11) who actively try to infiltrate the church and spread false teaching with evil intent (Rev 2v 20).

Scripture puts more weight on this than many Christians; we don't like to think the church is infiltrated by the devil (Acts 20v 29-30). False teachers and false prophets seek out 'prophetic' opportunities within and without the church to trumpet their lies. Think how rapidly the Gnostic teachers snapped at the heels of the early church. It is foolishness to think today it is any different. The path of least resistance always leads to syncretism; the price of spiritual purity is high, but the cost of compromise is higher still!

Dear friends, do not believe every spirit, but test the spirits to see whether they are from God, because many false prophets have gone out into the world.
(1 John 4v 1)

THE GIFT OF DISCERNMENT IS ESSENTIAL

We must take responsibility for our own spiritual health, learning to divide the Word of God for ourselves (2 Tim2 v 15).The discerning of spirits is an invaluable, even essential gift and should be prioritised in our prayers. We need it desperately in these confusing times (1 Cor 12v 9). This gift in others has rescued me from deception several times, and I seek it myself too. Simply put; we must hear God for ourselves. God's light and peace in our hearts is a good sign we are safe to proceed.

Just because we are fed something from the pulpit doesn't mean we have to swallow it wholesale (1 Thess 5v 21). I'm not encouraging rebellion, rather, healthy questioning. Even the greatest teachers are not infallible. No denomination has it all right; and most Christians have dipped into different streams at times for enrichment and balance in teaching. God only sees one true church, denominations were Man's idea!

Let's ask our gracious Lord and teacher to cleanse out of our minds and hearts any false teaching and to renew us with life-giving truth from His Word. Then we move on confidently and joyfully, earnestly desiring the gift of prophecy (1 Cor 1v 14).

Bible Studies

These studies are provided for both group and personal study purposes. They encourage a deeper biblical exploration of the themes exposed in this book. As such, they will bring added insight into God's purposes within the prophetic.

Bible study 1

Jonah 1v 1–3, 3v 1–10
Jonah the reluctant prophetic evangelist

(Prophetic Evangelism – chapter 7)

What is unique about Jonah's prophetic call from God, and distinct in the Old Testament?

What strikes you about the city wide call to repentance in Nineveh and their response. How does Jonah differ from other Old Testament prophets in his message to another nation?

What do we learn about God's heart for the nations through Jonah?

Who the gospel is for? Are there places, people groups or individuals we would struggle to go to even if God specifically asked us? Why would God choose someone who would be reluctant?

I make the point that Jonah is a 'type' of prophetic evangelist, what does this mean to you?

Do you feel comfortable with the prophetic ministry and see it as biblical (please read Prophetic Evangelism chapters 3 and 4)? If not, what queries do you have? Have you ever received a prophetic word or given one?

Referencing chapters 2, 3 and 4 describe what is different about an evangelist and a prophetic evangelist. Do you lean more towards prophet or evangelist?

Have you ever operated as a prophetic evangelist without realising it? Give examples.

Do you have a 'little' Jonah living inside you?

If so, how does he influence your decisions? How can he be exorcised from your heart?

Has God ever asked you to do something you didn't want to do? Discuss how you heard or saw God, try to describe the experience as accurately as possible. How were you sure it was God and not another voice? Re-read chapter 13 Four voices.)

What are the pitfalls of prophetic evangelism? (Chapter 8)

What does Jonah teach us (negatively) about what we shouldn't do when God speaks to us? Have we ever been guilty of any of the seven pitfalls of prophetic evangelism in chapter 8?

- **Rejecting the message, running from God**
- **Lonewolf syndrome**
- **Obeying under duress, an unwilling servant**
- **Selfish use of our gifts**
- **Ministering to people we don't love**
- **Ending up angry with God**
- **Self pity party**

What happens to our peace if we refuse to do what God has told us to? If we lose our peace we need to retrace our steps to the point we lost it, often here we discover the reason for our unease. Why is our peace so important; what dangers are inherent in carrying on without it? Is it possible to run away from God?

What measures can we put in place spiritually, relationally, practically, and physically to avoid these pitfalls? How can we get better at recognising immediately when we've started down this track? Is there one pitfall we are particularly susceptible to?

Pray for each other in twos to strengthen weak spots. Be aware that we need to shed any unhealthy spiritual influences as these will make it harder to obey God immediately. Re-read chapter 5 *False Prophecy – occult influences* if you need to repent. Follow through the four r's

- **Recognise**
- **Repent**
- **Renounce**
- **Resist**

Ask someone to hold you accountable for what you have repented of? God works through Godly human relationships to keep us on track. The Bible knows nothing of repentance without human accountability.

Bible study 2

(Prophetic Evangelism – chapter 11 and 12)

Jesus is poetry in motion, what do you particularly admire about Jesus' methods?

Discuss how Jesus utilises natural phenomenon, works with what is already happening and interacts with people.

In what ways did Jesus treat Nicodemus and the Samaritan woman differently?

He acknowledged their different starting points.

In what ways did Jesus treat them the same?

He is no respecter of persons (Acts 10 v 34). He's not impressed by status or repulsed by the outcast.

Live in the moment, flow with the Spirit

This sounds so spiritual but what does it mean, practically, to do this? How well do you 'flow' with the Spirit. Discuss a time when this might have happened and what it felt like.

Why do most human beings like formulae so much?

How can we avoid our methods crystallising until eventually they become obsolete? Why is it always easier to spot this happening to others than to ourselves? How do we keep our hunger to participate in the Holy Spirit's activity consistently high?

1. Be purposeful without rushing

How true is this statement, the fear of Man hurries and manipulates us whereas the fear of the Lord keeps us in step with Him? What are the things that cause us to rush? Why? e.g. self-doubt/ anxiety / self-consciousness / low self-esteem.

Are we agenda driven or people focussed? How do we get balance if we are target focussed? Are we so people focussed that we never bring a challenge?

2. Resist distractions

How do we know if we are dealing with a 'spiritual' distraction and not a genuine question or an urgent need? Role play one person trying to maintain eye contact and share the gospel and the other distracting and going off at tangents.

If we sense a 'spiritual interference' what can we do to counteract it? Is it rude to ignore a direct question if we want to stay on course with the gospel?

If 0 is not good at all the way up to 10 which is outstanding, indicate where you you are on this scale. Ask someone you trust to score you

Live in the moment, flow with the Spirit...   ☐ ☐

Being purposeful without rushing...   ☐ ☐

Resist distractions...   ☐ ☐

After two months and after several excursions into prophetic evangelism come back and see if your numbers have changed? What practical steps can we take, acknowledging our starting position, to step out in prophetic evangelism?

Is there someone confident we can go out with?

Pray for each other to be filled afresh with the Holy Spirit.

Bible study 3

Acts 11v 1–11, 8v 26–40, 27v 21–26
Peter, Philip and Paul, prophetic evangelists

(Prophetic Evangelism – chapter 16)

What similarities are there in the way God guides these prophetic evangelists?

Angels/visions/dreams/prophecy/pictures/other followers of Jesus.

What differences are there in how God speaks to these prophetic evangelists?

Discuss how God often speaks in a way that is personal and specific to what He is asking us to do.

Has God ever challenged your cultural prejudices like Peter, Philip or Paul?

Which of these three prophetic evangelists do you most identify with? What is it about his experiences that you most identify with? Have you ever been Spirit led like he was? Have you ever said or thought, 'I'll do anything but that Lord.' Why?

Discuss how we can discern God speaking, from other voices
(please read chapter 15 – Four voices)

- **God's voice**
- **Our own heart (voice)**
- **The devil**
- **Other people's hearts**

Give examples of hearing from all four of these.

Would we be willing to be led away from apparent 'success' to one person like Peter and Philip?

Look at the parable of the lost sheep. Discuss a kingdom (big picture) perspective rather than local church vision.

What is 'success' in prophetic evangelism?

(Whether we've covered all four gospel points/ conversations about Jesus/prayed for sickness?/left someone in a better place than we found them?)

Share a testimony of a time when God clearly directed you by spiritual means?

(However unspectacular or strange it may seem. Please suspend your incredulity if others share things you haven't experienced)

Should we expect supernatural guidance?

Why is it that clear guidance seems to come to those who are already in motion serving God? How can we best position ourselves to receive from God? (read Chapters 13 and 14)

Bible study 4

Revelation chapter 11v 1–12
Prophetic evangelism in the End Times

(Prophetic Evangelism – chapter 17)

When are the End Times?

Peter's preaching from Joel in Acts chapter 2

Why is it significant that the two witnesses prophesy and give testimony?

They have God's authority, yet their message is not received. What parallels can we see today?

Do the witnesses shy away from a hostile reaction?

They are willing to pay the ultimate price (Rev 12v 11).

How do the witnesses stay courageous?

Intimacy/partnership with the Holy Spirit/overcoming persecution/knowing the word of God etc.)

Have you ever engaged in this sort of evangelism? (read Chapter 18 – Ten Reasons why prophetic evangelism is for now)

If so, share your experiences in your group, one 'success' and one 'blunder'. What was good about it, what was challenging? Do you agree with the ten reasons below why prophetic evangelism is for now? If not, why?

(On a scale of 0-10, 0 being strongly disagree, 10 being strongly agree, and 5 being not sure, write a number next to each of the following):

Prophetic evangelism:

1. **demonstrates a personal God** ☐
2. **brings absolutes into a subjective world** ☐
3. **can pivot to any number of different gifts** ☐
4. **speaks to a generation hungry for the supernatural** ☐
5. **can operate in almost every situation** ☐
6. **can be 'under the radar'** ☐
7. **requires us to walk closely with Jesus** ☐
8. **can grab people's attention** ☐
9. **is exciting and faith building for us** ☐
10. **glorifies Jesus** ☐

Suggestions: Set a time and date with your group to try some prophetic evangelism. Go for a 'prophetic walk' and see where God leads you and/or to whom. Ask God, ahead of time, to show you what and/or who you should look for. Pray for each other to receive/grow in this gift.

FEEDBACK to each other, and go again, rejoicing!

Further reading

Through The Tunnel – Free At Last

Daniel Holland, PUSH Publishing

"Staggering across my bedroom I opened the cupboard. Lifting another hidden bottle of vodka I took a huge slug. The feeling of being out of my depth was overwhelming but I thought I knew what I must do. *The wedding must be cancelled, there is no other way; tomorrow I must tell Beck*".

The words on the back cover naturally draw the reader in.
Jennifer Rees Larcombe calls this "a vital resource for people in the Christian healing ministry". As you read this book you know you have in your hands something of considerable value – a real man's flesh and blood story – and a story that ends in blessing and in the glory of Jesus. But what a journey to get there!

Daniel Holland is quite clear that this journey is through an emotional, mental and spiritual tunnel, very dark in places. Holland enjoyed what was in many respects a conventional Christian upbringing and a happy childhood. Yet at the age of nine something happened that altered the course of his life. After this his life underwent a number of emotional and spiritual convulsions. Hurts were buried deep within. Hurts that needed healing were instead buried, only to manifest themselves in later life in emotional and mental torment.

A book that prompts reflective thought and encourages readers to think deeply on the question of healing and God's purposes in hugely difficult circumstances. It underscores the truth of Scripture; "all things work together for good, to those who love the Lord" (Romans 8:28). Holland's life and his present work bear out this truth.

Available as a paperback via Christian Publications International.
Also available as a Kindle (e-book) edition via Amazon at
https://www.amazon.co.uk/Through-Tunnel-Free-at-Last/dp/0955378346
at £3.97.

Books by Rev Alex Jacob, CEO of CMJ

100 Days with Luke
100 Days with Acts
60 Days with Romans

Easy to digest studies, forming a valuable trilogy. Rev Alex Jacob opens up two books by Luke, together with Romans by Paul.

Each day contains a passage from the book being studied as devotional bible studies. Each has a brief reflection from the writer and finally a "to consider" question. Ideal for both private and group study.

The material has been adopted by some churches as Lent Course material, with the added value of helping build up a basic set of mini-commentaries.

This series makes life easy for the busy house group leader, or church leader, by providing its own set of discussion questions. It can also accompany a preaching series.

Christian Publications International
www.christian-publications-int.com

Recent titles from CPI

Heartreach – The ongoing story of God's grace in a challenging environment

Professor Mel Richardson, MBE

The amazing, gritty, adventure story of God's grace through Project Dengke (Tibet). A key recurring theme is reaching out with practical love and kindness to those in real need, such as leprosy patients and youngsters in extreme poverty. The impossible is demonstrated possible. Whether building a Friendship Centre in the most sensitive region of China /Tibet, or a self-proclaimed "Living Buddha" wanting his monks to be Christians, be prepared to be amazed and encouraged – irrespective of whether you have faith yourself.

(endorsed by Sir Ranulph Fiennes and Rt Hon Baroness Cox (Caroline Cox))

Revelations of Jesus Christ – a devotional study from the book of Revelation

Philip Wren

In this delightful and challenging study Philip Wren reveals the inner coherence of Revelation, the 'Bible book that concludes the testimony of Jesus and reveals to us the future triumph of Christ'. Revelation was written for ordinary people, not for theologians, and this study highlights the major themes without over-complicating the subject.

With a broad appeal as a useful and practical study for both pastors and the general Christian reader.

22 Hebrew key names of God form 22 chapter headings. Each chapter explores the corresponding chapter in Revelation.

Three Days and Three Nights
– That Changed the World

David Serle and Peter Sammons

Sub-titled '*Do the Biblical accounts of the Passion and the Resurrection Agree?*' this book sets out to demonstrate beyond reasonable doubt that they do! Matthew, Mark and Luke tell us that Jesus' crucifixion was after His Passover meal. John tells us that Jesus was arrested (and therefore crucified) before the Passover meal. How do we resolve this apparent discrepancy? If Jesus was crucified on "Good Friday" and resurrected on Sunday morning, how should we understand His specific prophecy that His body would be entombed for "three days and three nights"?

These and numerous other practical questions relating to Holy Week are explored and clarified in this valuable study.

Christian Publications International
www.christian-publications-int.com

PE4h09/21